A Critique of the Theory of Abrogation

JASSER AUDA

Translated and Edited by
Adil Salahi

THE ISLAMIC FOUNDATION

A Critique of the Theory of Abrogation

First published in England by
Kube Publishing Ltd
Markfield Conference Centre,
Ratby Lane, Markfield,
Leicestershire, LE67 9SY
United Kingdom
Tel: +44 (0) 1530 249230 Fax: +44 (0) 1530 249656
Website: www.kubepublishing.com
Email: info@kubepublishing.com

Cataloguing in-Publication Data is available from the British Library

ISBN 978-0-86037-730-6 Paperback
ISBN 978-0-86037-760-3 Ebook

Cover Design: Nasir Cadir
Typesetting: Nasir Cadir

Printed by: Imak, Turkey.

Contents

Introduction

A RULE OF FALSE logic has pervaded intellectual and philosophical methodologies, which we may call 'the rule of inevitable false dualism'. It simply involves that any philosophical question may be presented as a choice between two logical conclusions and there can be no third alternative. Debate ensues between two extreme opposites and each debater tries hard to prove their point and refute their opponent's argument.

For example, there is a long-drawn debate between the advocates of objectivism, who maintain that things have natural realities that we can arrive at through consciousness, and the advocates of subjectivism, who claim that it is impossible to arrive at the reality of things. People simply have certain mental pictures of things. Each side makes certain arguments in support of their principle. We note that there are few attempts to come up with a theory that combines the facts of both sides, such as those who speak of 'a reality with a social subjectivity' as an alternative to both views. These try to combine all that is right in all views and reconcile the seemingly contradictory arguments.

Students of philosophy argue about another supposedly inevitable dualism even though it is false, namely, the dualism of science and religion. Many people imagine that the two are mutually contradictory. Indeed, this dualism appeared in our Islamic heritage under the heading 'the contradiction between reason and revelation' or 'the contradiction between the rational view and religious text'. This occurred in spite of the strong emphasis Islam lays on the bond between faith and intellectual reasoning, which is well known to all. Many people imagine that they have to make an inevitable choice between what belongs to religion and what belongs to science. Other correlative choices are between the material and the metaphysical; personal interest and morality; the material and the spiritual; and other opposites that are by no means mutually exclusive.

Science and religion may be mutually contradictory in a particular area or dimension. For example, religion gives top position to its texts, while science accords that position to experience and observation. However, who can say that the Islamic faith, and its central belief, is not based on experience and observation? Who can claim that intellectual consideration of scientific findings has nothing to do with the Divine text? The Qur'ānic method of proving God's existence and belief – in anything – is based on observation and contemplation. God says in the Qur'ān: '*Say*: "*Consider all that there is in the heavens and the earth*."' (10: 101) '*No fault will you see in what the Lord of Grace creates. Turn up your eyes: can you see any flaw? Then look again, and again: your vision will come back to you dull and weary*.' (67: 3–4) Indeed, Ibn Taymiyyah was absolutely right when he chose for his voluminous work on logic and philosophy the title: 'Prevention of contradiction between reason and revelation, or the consistency between authentic religious texts and clearly rational views'. Moreover, religion and science are mutually complementary in several other areas, such as that both aim at the achievement of human happiness, and both attach central importance to the origin of life, the system of existence, and so on.

We may also consider that mind as an abstract and as matter, which is subject to our senses, are mutually complementary, rather than contradictory. If we extend our area of consideration beyond the domain of the five senses, we realise that the most recent theories of comprehension and the brain suggest that mind and matter have mutual influence on each other. Numerous examples of the interaction between mind and matter are given in contemporary sciences, such as having a hunch that leads to a fact without there being any material evidence pointing to it, or a dream that comes true, or the effect of spiritual and psychological factors on patients. We only need to think of the effect of *ruqyah*, which is a supplication, in speeding up a patient's recovery.

Islamic legal theory (*uṣūl al-fiqh*) – the different schools of which represent the philosophy of Islamic legislation – was not immune to the different philosophical systems and their false assumptions. A number of false dualisms appeared in some theories of *uṣūl al-fiqh* leading to long-drawn debates and differences. Yet some scholars of legal theories were aware that it was possible in each such case to reconcile opposed views within a creative and useful framework.

For example, scholars of legal theory differ concerning the acceptability of certain secondary sources as evidence or as the basis of rulings. Some would consider a certain source as acceptable evidence pointing to a particular conclusion or ruling, while others would consider it unacceptable or 'false', in the legal theorists' parlance. If a source of evidence is acceptable then it may serve as a basis for a ruling, while a 'false' source is essentially unacceptable under any circumstances, and as such no ruling can be based on it. Representatives of this view include al-Shāfi'ī's *Buṭlān al-istiḥsān*, or 'The invalidity of subtle analogy'; Dāwūd's *Ibṭāl al-qiyās*, or 'Refutation of analogy'; Ibn al-Rāwandī's *Ibṭāl al-tawātur*, or 'Refuting recurrence'; the disagreement between the Mālikī and the Shāfi'ī schools on whether the actions of the people of Madīnah serve as evidence for rulings or not; and the disagreement between the Ẓāhirōs, Ja'farīs and Zaydīs on one side and the rest of the *fiqh* schools on the other side on whether analogy is acceptable as evidence or not.

For example, the practice or the unanimity of the people of Madīnah is a full source of evidence according to the Mālikī school of *fiqh*. Imām Mālik determined many questions on its basis, such as the unanimity of the people of Madīnah in explaining certain verses of the Qur'ān. He considered such practice or unanimity a standard by which greater weight is given to certain Hadiths of the category of *āḥād* (narrated by single reporters). Imam al-Shāfi'ī rejected the very concept of giving the people of Madīnah or their practice any special legislative status, arguing that it could open the door to claiming such status for the unanimity of the people of other cities.[1]

Some scholars, such as Ibn Taymiyyah and Ibn al-Qayyim, take a different view, which does not consider the question as an inevitable dualism. They accept the

1. Muḥammad ibn Idrīs al-Shāfi'ī, *al-Risālah*, p. 158.

practice of the people of Madīnah as a basis in considering certain questions, although they themselves belong to the Ḥanbalī school of *fiqh*, which rejects the idea of considering such practice as a source of evidence. Ibn Taymiyyah, for example, considers the unanimity of the people of Madīnah, the Prophet's city, as a sort of collective narration of the Prophet's Sunnah. As such, it is treated as another narration that may even be more authentic than narrations by single reporters. This is a fine and logical solution that puts this source of evidence in a broader perspective that enables us to benefit from what is positive and useful of it, rather than confining it to the restriction of a dualism that either totally accepts or rejects it.[2]

Let us take another example of false dualism from legal theory, which is known as 'the concept of opposite implications' (*mafhūm al-mukhālafah*). All main schools of legal theory, apart from the Ḥanafī school, consider the meaning of the wording of a text to be of two parts: agreement and disagreement. Thus, the concept of disagreement means that if the wording of a text confirms a particular ruling, then according to the concept of opposite implications, the same wording confirms its opposite. In other words, the presence of a particular fact means logically the absence of its opposite. The *fiqh* schools that adopt the concept of opposite implications divide it into five categories: name, description, condition, extent and number. Thus, the mention of any of these five categories in the text of the Qur'ān or a Hadith means that its opposite is non-existent or false. The Ḥanafī scholars reject this logic, but their position is not based on rejecting the concept of false dualisms. They consider that

2. Aḥmad 'Abd al-Ḥalīm Ibn Taymiyyah, *Kutub wa Rasā'il wa Fatāwā Ibn Taymiyyah fī al-Fiqh*, vol. 20, pp. 123, 133, 163, 203 and 283.

a single reason behind a religious text cannot include two rulings at the same time.[3] Yet this is another false dualism.

For example, *fiqh* scholars discuss the adjective 'pastured' in the Hadith: 'Zakat is due on pastured animals'.[4] According to the concept of opposite implications, cows that are not taken to pasture are not liable for Zakat in the view of the majority of scholars,[5] even though they represent a property liable to growth. This is clearly contrary to the very purpose of Zakat. An example of the 'description' category and the application of the concept of opposite implications occurs in the following Qur'ānic verse: '*Any of you who, owing to circumstances, is not in a position to marry a free believing woman may marry a believing maiden from among those whom your right hands possess.*' (4: 25) The description here is the word 'believing', which refers to women and maidens. Al-Shāfi'ī considers belief a condition for the validity of marriage. Hence, operating the concept of opposite implications, al-Shāfi'ī considers marriage with non-believers unlawful in all situations. By contrast, the Ḥanafī scholars, who do not accept the concept of opposite implications, consider that a Muslim man may marry a woman who is a believer or an unbeliever. They argue that the adjective 'believing' in the verse does not necessarily negate unbelievers. Thus, they reject the false dualism.

In the category of 'condition' we may give the following example of inevitable dualism. God says in the Qur'ān: '*If they [meaning divorced women] are with child, maintain them until they have delivered their burden.*' (65: 6) Implementing the concept of opposite implications, scholars say that if a divorced woman is not pregnant, then she does

3. Muḥammad Abū Zuhrah, *Uṣūl al-Fiqh*, pp. 136–9.
4. Yūsuf al-Qaradāwī, *Fiqh al-Zakāt*, vol. 1, p. 240.
5. Ibid., p. 141.

not have the right to maintenance by her divorcing husband. This is contrary to the understood meaning that when a man chooses to divorce his wife, he bears certain financial responsibility towards her. The Ḥanafī scholars disagree because they reject the concept of opposite implications,[6] not because of the contradiction with the understood meaning.

An example of the 'extent' category is found in the following verse detailing rulings applicable to fasting: '*Eat and drink until you can see the white streak of dawn against the blackness of the night.*' (2: 187) This verse makes clear that eating and drinking are permissible until the specified time, but not after that. The Ḥanafī school shares the same ruling, but the Ḥanafī scholars consider that the verse mentions eating and drinking as primary actions, and that they are specifically meant, not as a result of the concept of opposite implications.[7]

The concept of opposite implications is also applied to 'number'. Thus, when a verse of the Qur'ān or a Hadith mentions a particular number, then all other numbers are, according to this concept, unacceptable. It is not possible that any other number, even ones mentioned in other verses or Hadiths, can replace that specified number in the same context. Examples are found in the Hadiths concerning Zakat and specify thresholds for liability to Zakat in different types of property. These thresholds, specifying numbers, may differ in different narrations or Hadiths. Most scholars resort to the solution of specifying a particular number and rejecting others, either through considering a particular text weightier on balance or through inevitable choice even though different narrations are equally authentic, or through abrogation even though the abrogated text is confirmed. All

6. Abū Zuhrah, *Uṣūl al-Fiqh*, p. 143.
7. Ibid., p. 144.

this is not religiously required. This book is a critique of such an approach, which is based on dualism, its reasoning and conclusions.

All *fiqh* schools exclude figurative descriptions from the concept of opposite implications, as well as any effect of the application of this concept that is in contradiction with other texts.[8] However, the cited examples show that the very concept of dualism presents us with a type of choice between two alternatives that, in my view, represents faulty reasoning which both lacks evidence and is unnecessary. Indeed, such fallacies lead to rigidity in *fiqh* and contribute to the formation of a mentality that does not leave room for a middle ground between opposite choices or the reconciliation of varying meanings. Such dualism in reading religious texts also limits the flexibility of rulings as they apply to changing circumstances and it restricts the ability of *fiqh* to address new circumstances and conditions. Furthermore, it prevents religious texts from guiding such flexibility, which is a main objective of such texts.

When the concept of opposite implications was applied to number, as has been mentioned earlier, in some cases of Zakat it resulted in what was called 'contradiction' between a number of Hadiths mentioning specific numbers of what should be paid in Zakat. There were marginal differences in the numbers mentioned in authentic Hadiths.[9] As we shall see, scholars found themselves having to claim that other numbers mentioned in authentic Hadiths were abrogated. Such claims were made only to ensure consistency in the application of the concept of opposite implications to numbers.

8. Ibid., p. 140.
9. Al-Qaradāwī, *Fiqh al-Zakāt*, vol. 1, p. 182.

The amount of Zakat payable on camels as specified in the instructions the Prophet (peace be upon him) ordered to be written to Abū Bakr, 'Alī and 'Amr ibn Ḥazm varied.[10] Because of these differences, scholars differed as to which numbers they should adopt and which they should abandon on the basis of the concept of opposite implications. A few scholars tried to reconcile the relevant reports. Al-Ṭabarī, for example, reconciled all these reports by stating that a scholar is free to determine which number to apply in estimating the amount of Zakat due.[11] In his highly distinguished book, *Fiqh al-*Zakat, Shaykh Yūsuf al-Qaradāwī reconciled the numbers by stating that the Zakat collector may apply any of the numbers on the basis of the financial status of the Zakat payer.[12] Such types of reconciliation are better, as a well-known rule of *fiqh* states that; 'It is better to enforce a religious text than to discard it'.

If we take a broader look at the religious objectives of the whole issue of Zakat, disregarding inevitable dualisms and their mutual effects of weight or contradiction, we will not need to deal with or reconcile any contradiction. It is well known that one of the objectives of Zakat is to take a donation, or *ṣadaqah*, from people who have more than the threshold of Zakat and have held their property for a year, which means that they have over a certain standard of wealth. This donation is given to the poor, the needy, insolvent debtors and other beneficiaries of Zakat. This broad perspective presupposes taking into consideration the amount of wealth and its growth, as well as how rich any individual is, regardless of whether his cattle is pastured or

10. Muḥammad ibn Ismā'īl al-Bukhārī, *Ṣaḥīḥ*.
11. Muḥammad ibn Jarīr al-Ṭabarī, *Jāmi' al-Bayān 'an Ta'wīl Āy al-Qur'ān*, vol. 5, p. 401.
12. Al-Qaradāwī, *Fiqh al-Zakāt*, vol. 1, p. 184.

not, her gold is circular or not, the underground resources are solid minerals or liquid ones, the agricultural produce is wheat, barley or rubber, and regardless of all other details to which Islamic legislation does not pay much attention in the first place.

As we shall see, the objectives of Islamic legislation include ensuring mutual social security, making matters easy for people, and ensuring law and order in society. Therefore, numbers and shapes of property may differ, but should not and do not affect the duty of Zakat or its fulfilment of its goals and aims.

The aforementioned logical premises and brief examples merely serve as an introduction to this book. I feel that what I am tackling has an important and essential role in the process of contemporary Islamic revival. My subject presents a methodological critique of the theory of abrogation, which is often misunderstood and wrongly applied by scholars of early and modern days.

I have written on this subject on more than one occasion, tackling it from different angles and within different contexts. This book brings together what I have written earlier and presents my ideas through examples that point to various questions to which the theory of abrogation, in the sense of annulment, was applied in order to arrive at confirmed and settled rulings. Yet we will see that this sense of abrogation is by no means valid from an Islamic point of view.

The theory of abrogation is similar to that of dualism, which we have already mentioned, in the fact that it has a long heritage that has been transferred from one generation to another. This heritage is represented in the branch disciplines of Islamic studies known as *al-Nāsikh wa al-Mansūkh* (the abrogating and the abrogated texts),

Mukhtalaf al-Ḥadīth (Hadiths that are at variance) and *Ḥall al-Ta'āruḍ* (reconciliation of contradictory statements). This is a heritage that has been greatly impacted by inevitable dualisms, which is wholly unnecessary in the same way that a full picture does not have to be only in black and white. This book will show that in every question where contradiction was assumed, some meticulous scholars have discussed it in detail, refuting the idea of contradiction and abrogation, drawing the picture in all its splendid colours.

This humble effort tries to paint a general picture of Islamic law, through the discussion of this subject. It aims to present in full colour, not in black and white, what we understand of its meanings. This provides us with a splendid picture and a positive way forward. I seek God's help and place my trust in Him. To Him belong all knowledge and all grace. To Him I turn and pray to grant me success.

Chapter One

Objectives of Islamic Law: Concepts and Aims

IT IS IMPORTANT to start by defining certain terms and concepts which we will be using in this work. The first thing we need to clarify is what we mean by *maqāṣid al-sharī'ah* or 'objectives of Islamic law'. This is defined as 'the results that God, the Legislator, wants to be achieved through His legislation and rulings'.[1] We know these results through study, that is, by the efforts of scrupulous scholars to understand religious texts, putting them together and deducing what they aim to fulfil and achieve.

The 'objectives' have many divisions and classifications, the most comprehensive of which is provided by contemporary scholars who write in this field. They agree that there are three levels of objectives: general, special and partial.[2]

1. Muḥammad al-Ṭāhir Ibn 'Āshūr, *Maqāṣid al-Sharī'ah al-Islāmiyyah*, p. 183.
2. Nu'mān Jughaym, *Ṭuruq al-Kashf 'an Maqāṣid al-Shāri'*, pp. 26–35. We find in this book different classifications, taken from different angles.

The general objectives refer to the purposes addressed in all aspects of Islamic law, or in numerous and varied aspects of it, such as tolerance, removal of hardship, justice, freedom, agreement with human nature, consistency with natural laws, the preservation of the Muslim community and its system, and so on.[3]

The general objectives include the five or six well-known essentials (*ḍarūrāt*, sing. *ḍarūrah*), which mean the safeguarding of faith, life, reason, offspring, property and family honour. The basis of classifying these as essentials is that they are considered essential to the continuity of human life itself. Scholars say that the safeguarding of these is the aim of every Divine faith.[4] Thus, at the level of essentials, the objectives are matters of life and death.

At the level of needs (*ḥājiyyāt*), the objectives are less necessary for human life. They include matters like marriage, commerce, roads, means of transport and consumer goods, in our contemporary parlance. These interests or needs do not rise to the level of essentials unless they become non-existent in a particular society, causing a general crisis that may lead to the loss of the essentials. At the level of enhancements (*taḥsīniyyāt*), the objectives are in a lesser category than needs. In modern terms, they refer to what adds to people's comfort, but can be dispensed with.[5]

The special objectives are certain interests and meanings addressed in a particular section of Islamic law, such as the objectives of taking care of children's interests and preventing harm being caused to women in the section on family law; the objectives of crime prevention and establishing the truth in the penal law; and the objectives of

3. Ibn 'Ashur, *Maqāṣid al-Sharī'ah*, p. 183.
4. Ibrāhīm ibn Mūsā al-Shāṭibī, *al-Muwāfaqāt*, vol. 3, p. 5.
5. Ibid., vol. 3, p. 17.

clarity, prevention of uncertainty and cheating in financial transactions, and so on.

Partial objectives are defined as the underlying purposes considered by the Legislator in a particular ruling on certain details,[6] such as the objective of ensuring truth and accuracy in determining the number and qualities of witnesses, or the objective of removing hardship in the exemption from fasting of those who find fasting too hard, and so on.

Scholars of the early generations and of modern days also discuss the objectives of faith, giving the matter terms that may differ from the 'objectives of beliefs' in form but agree in content. They speak of the 'secrets (*asrār*), wisdom (*ḥikam*), purposes (*aghrāḍ*), beauties (*maḥāsin*), and qualities (*manāqib*)' related to the right beliefs such as belief in God, His Books, His Messengers, the Last Day and His Will, as well as God's attributes and actions, and so on.[7]

If we look at the history of the term *al-maqāṣid* we find that Imam al-Juwaynī, one of the founders of this discipline, sometimes refers to the objectives of Islamic law as 'general interests'.[8] Abū Ḥāmid al-Ghazālī considers all three types of objectives as part of unspecified interests (*al-maṣāliḥ al-mursalah*).[9] Al-Ṭūfī defines interest as 'what leads to the fulfilment of the objective of the Legislator by way of worship, not by way of habit'.[10] The same is expressed by

6. Jughaym, *Ṭuruq al-Kashf 'an Maqāṣid al-Shāri'*, p. 28.
7. See: Muḥammad ibn 'Alī al-Ḥakīm al-Tirmidhī, *Ithbat al-'Ilal*; Shah Walī Allāh al-Dihlawī, *Ḥujjat Allāh al-Bālighah*; Abū Ḥāmid al-Ghazālī, *Shifā' al-Ghalīl*.
8. 'Abd al-Malik ibn 'Abd Allāh al-Juwaynī, *Ghiyāth al-Umam fī Iltiyāth al-Ẓulam*.
9. See al-Ghazālī, *Al-Mustaṣfā*, vol. 1, p. 172; Fakhr al-Dīn Muḥammad ibn 'Umar al-Rāzī, *al-Maḥṣūl*, vol. 5, p. 222; 'Alī ibn Muḥammad al-Āmidī, *al-Aḥkām*, vol. 4, p. 286.
10. Sulaymān ibn 'Abd al-Qawī al-Ṭūfī, *al-Ta'yīn fī Sharḥ al-Arba'īn*, p. 239.

al-Qarafi as he said: 'A rule: Islam does not consider an objective except what leads to the fulfilment of a proper purpose that ensures an interest or prevents harm'.[11] Tāj al-Dīn al-Subkī said: 'Shaykh al-Islām 'Izz al-Dīn ibn 'Abd al-Salām considers that the purpose of the entire body of *fiqh* is to serve people's interests and ensure the prevention of harm. Were anyone to question him he would have summed it all up in serving people's interests, because the prevention of harm is part of it'. Al-'Izz said: 'Whoever studies the objectives of Islamic law in serving interests and preventing harm will arrive at a conclusion that such-and-such interest must not be ignored and that such-and-such harm must not be done, even though there is no text, unanimity or analogy suggesting this. Indeed, the mere understanding of Islamic law requires this'.[12] The objectives of Islamic law and interests in general are, according to many scholars of legal theory, two terms expressing the same meaning.

Defining the Legislator's objectives by the text is a matter of scholarly discretion, but it has a basis in what God's Messenger (peace be upon him) approved of in his Companions' understanding and deeds. A case in point is reported in the two authentic Hadith anthologies of al-Bukhārī and Muslim, as well as other anthologies. Ibn 'Umar reports: 'When the Prophet (peace be upon him) came back to Madīnah after [the encounter with] the allies of Quraysh (*al-Aḥzāb*), he told us: "Let none of you pray *'aṣr* except at the quarters of Banī Qurayẓa". When *'aṣr* was due, many were still on the way. Some of them said: "We shall not pray until we reach there". Others said: "We shall pray, because he did not mean that literally [meaning that he only

11. Aḥmad ibn Idrīs al-Qarafī, *al-Dhakhīrah*, vol. 5, p. 478.
12. 'Abd al-Wahhāb ibn 'Alī al-Subkī, *al-Ashbāh wa al-Naẓā'ir*, vol. 1, p. 12.

stressed that we should make haste]". This was mentioned to the Prophet (peace be upon him) and he did not take issue with any of them'.[13] In Muslim's narration: 'Others said: "We shall not pray except where God's Messenger (peace be upon him) ordered us to pray, even though we miss out the prayer time"'.[14]

This Hadith speaking of offering the *'aṣr* prayer at the Qurayẓa quarters is a basic principle allowing firstly the determination of the objective of a particular text on the basis of one's understanding, and secondly the permissibility of defining practical rulings according to this determined objective, even though it goes against the wording of the text. The Prophet's Companions who said that the Prophet merely intended that they should make haste, and not that they must pray at the Qurayẓa quarters, actually disobeyed the apparent meaning of the order when they offered their prayer on the way. The other Companions, who insisted on waiting until they had arrived at the Qurayẓa quarters, even though it would be after the *'aṣr* time had lapsed, took the order literally. They left the reason for this order to God and His Messenger. The fact that the Prophet approved both actions means that both methods are permissible.

Scholars' comments on this Hadith differ according to their schools of legal theory and whether they lean towards establishing rulings on the basis of the apparent meaning of a text or its objective. However, the majority of scholars lean towards the actions of those who acted on the basis of the objective behind the order. Ibn al-Qayyim sums up their view as follows: 'Both parties will be rewarded according to their intentions. However, those who prayed on the way achieved both good actions: obeying the order to make haste

13. Al-Bukhārī, *Ṣaḥīḥ*, vol. 1, p. 321.
14. Muslim ibn al-Ḥajjāj, *Ṣaḥīḥ*, vol. 3, p. 1391.

and obeying the order to offer prayers on time... The fact that the Prophet (peace be upon him) did not take issue with those who delayed the prayer is due to the fact that they have the clear excuse of adhering to the literal meaning of the order.'[15] Thus, Ibn al-Qayyim considers making haste, which is the objective understood by some of the Prophet's Companions from the context, not the wording of the Hadith, to be a religious order in its own right and to be obeyed. He also considers that the others, who adhered to the literal meaning of the order, are excused for basing their action on their understanding, which to him was incorrect.

The adherents of the Ẓāhirī school, of older generations and more recent ones, do not consider inner meaning or ultimate aims. This is not part of their logic. Ibn Ḥazm expresses their view in his usual style: 'Had we been there on the day of Banī Qurayẓa, we would not have prayed *'aṣr* until we had reached there, even if that had been after midnight.'[16] This view is consistent with their methodology of legal theory, based on taking all texts at face value, without looking at their objectives or contexts.

This Hadith and similar ones represent a basis for what we present in this book, namely, to deduce rulings on the basis of the objectives of texts, relate rulings to such objectives and understand them within their framework, rather than to claim abrogation of texts without proper evidence confirming either the principle or its application. In looking at the objectives with such methodology we have several aims:

---

15. Ibn al-Qayyim's view is quoted by Ibn Ḥajar, *Fatḥ al-Bārī*, vol. 7, p. 410. See also Ibn Taymiyyah, *Kutub wa Rasā'il wa Fatāwā*, vol. 20, p. 252; Ismā'īl Ibn Kathīr, *Tafsīr al-Qur'ān al-'Aẓīm*, vol. 1, p. 548; Muḥammad ibn 'Alī al-Shawkānī, *Nayl al-Awṭār*, vol. 4, p. 11.
16. 'Alī ibn Aḥmad Ibn Ḥazm, *al-Iḥkām fī Uṣūl al-Aḥkām*, vol. 3, p. 291.

Firstly, this book aims to preserve the flexibility of Islamic *fiqh* and its ability to address changing circumstances and times, so that it can ensure people's interests, taking into consideration 'changes of time, place, conditions, people, intentions and results', as Ibn al-Qayyim puts it. It may be right to enforce the apparent meanings of fatwas when all these dimensions remain the same. However, when time brings with it fundamentally different situations and practicalities, as is the case in our present time with regard to a very large number of issues and questions, we must not allow literalism to lead to hardship or harm that the objectives of Islamic law do not allow. Having cited the above-mentioned dimensions, Ibn al-Qayyim goes on to say:

> The essential basis of Islamic law is wisdom and serving people's interests in this present life and in the life to come. In all its parts and aspects, Islamic law ensures justice, deals with compassion, is based on wisdom and protects people's interests. Therefore, whatever moves away from justice towards injustice, from compassion towards its opposite, from protecting interests to causing harm or from wisdom to folly does not belong to Islamic law, even though it may be pushed into it through interpretation.[17]

There is no basis for any interpretation that contradicts the essentials of justice, compassion, wisdom and protection or safeguard of interest. All these four concepts, and other previously mentioned objectives, are fundamental factors and serve as standards determining the validity of interpretation and *ijtihād*: that is, scholarly effort and discretion.

---

17. Ibn al-Qayyim, *I'lām al-Muwaqqi'īn 'an Rabb al-'Ālamīn*, vol. 3, pp. 14–15.

Secondly, this book aims to enforce all religious texts regardless of what people imagine of 'contradiction' or 'variance' between them. In doing so, we implement the basic rule of legal theory, which is indeed a rule of faith, that says: 'It is better to enforce a religious text than to discard it.' How is it possible, from the point of view of methodology or faith, to discard a definitive text in God's book or in authentic Hadiths, particularly if such discarding is based on personal opinion and the claim that another text has more weight, even though all such texts are highly authentic? And how is it possible to discard such a text, even though it may be a definitive verse of the Qur'ān, claiming that it is abrogated when there is no evidence to confirm such an abrogation by God, the Legislator? This book does not reject either concept of some texts having more weight or being abrogated, but it limits them to a small number of cases and suggests clear conditions for enforcing them.

Thirdly, another aim of this book is to contribute to the efforts of scholars to establish the objectives of Islamic law as a common goal to serve all Muslims. It also contributes to their efforts to limit differences between them in matters of detail. Legal differences are a natural result of people's different nature, understanding and mental faculties, and they reflect an aspect of Islamic law itself. However, since the objectives are closer to the basic principles of Islamic law than traditional methodological assumptions, such as secondary and detailed evidence, then relating differences to such objectives is more effective in reducing differences and fanatic adherence to particular schools of *fiqh* or methodology.

Fourthly, this book aims to serve Islam, particularly in countries where Muslims are a minority community, through the presentation of the rulings of Islamic law in the light of their aims and objectives. This is closer to rational methodology, which has gained increased weight in our present time. Rational methodology requires that rulings and legislation must be consistent with their defined aims, values and legitimate objectives, not with literal interpretation or with the desires of those in authority, whoever they may be.

However, this book takes into consideration a particular controlling factor that represents an important religious objective, namely, that some Islamic rulings are related purely to worship. We establish this objective and clarify how it relates to the belief in what is beyond the reach of human perception, and the limitations of the human intellect in comparison with God's absolute knowledge.

Chapter Two

Internal Contradiction or Mutual Exclusion by a Scholar

1. Mutual exclusion or contradiction

MUTUAL EXCLUSION, or *ta'āruḍ* in Arabic, means that two things contribute to the action of exclusion. It is as if they stand in opposition to each other so that each represents an obstacle stopping the other. In the Qur'ān: '*Do not allow your oaths in the name of God to become an obstacle to your being kind and God-fearing, or to promoting peace among people. God hears all and knows all.*' (2: 224) This means that people should not make their oaths by God an obstacle to doing what brings them closer to God.[1] In *fiqh* terminology, the word is used when two pieces of religious evidence, such as two verses of the Qur'ān, two Hadiths or two cases of analogy, block each other. Scholars of logic, legal theory and Hadith are all agreed on an important principle, which is to differentiate

1. 'Abd al-Majīd al-Sawsawah, *Minhāj al-Tawfīq wa al-Tarjīḥ Bayn Mukhtalaf al-Ḥadīth*, pp. 45–6.

between two types of mutual exclusion, even though they call them by different names.

The first type is contradiction within the same matter,[2] which is also called logical contradiction,[3] or logical opposition,[4] or real contradiction.[5]

The second type is contradiction in a scholar's view,[6] or a scholar's mind.[7] It is also called apparent contradiction[8] or variance.[9] Different scholars use different names.

Al-Sarakhsī defines logical contradiction, or internal contradiction, as follows: 'Two equal arguments stand in opposition in such a way that each one of them denotes the opposite of what is denoted by the other, such as permissibility or prohibition; negation or confirmation.'[10] Ibn Qudāmah and Abū Ḥāmid al-Ghazālī define it as meaning the term 'contradiction'.[11] Al-Ghazālī explains contradiction in logical terminology, saying: 'Everything manifestly has an opposite that varies from it as positive and negative. If they are either true or false, they are called mutually contradictory.'[12] This means that if either of them is true the other is necessarily false, and if one area is white the other is necessarily and logically black. Philosophers outlined certain conditions for contradiction between two things, stipulating 'unity in time, place, application, force, action, totality, part

2. Al-Shāṭibī, *al-Muwāfaqāt*, vol. 4, p. 128.
3. Al-Ghazālī, *al-Mustaṣfā*, vol. 1, p. 279.
4. Al-Ghazālī, *Maḥakk al-Naẓar*, p. 27.
5. Al-Sawsawah, *Minhāj al-Tawfīq wa al-Tarjīḥ*, p. 59.
6. Al-Shāṭibī, *al-Muwāfaqāt*, vol. 4, p. 129.
7. Ibn Taymiyyah, *Kutub wa Rasā'il wa Fatāwā*, vol. 19, p. 131.
8. Muṣṭafā Zayd, *al-Naskh fī al-Qur'ān al-Karīm*, vol. 1, p. 169.
9. 'Abd al-Raḥmān al-Suyūṭī, *Tadrīb al-Rāwī*, vol. 2, p. 192.
10. Muḥammad ibn Aḥmad al-Sarakhsī, *Uṣūl al-Sarakhsī*, vol. 2, p. 12.
11. 'Abd Allāh Ibn Qudāmah, *Rawḍat al-Nāẓir*, p. 208; al-Ghazālī, *al-Mustaṣfā*, vol. 1, p. 279.
12. Al-Ghazālī, *Maqāṣid al-Falāsifah*, p. 62.

and condition'. The consequence of all these is that the two statements must not be different in anything at all other than negation and confirmation. Thus, one of them negates what the other confirms as applied to the same thing, without any difference.'[13] This means that the two questions are of the same meaning and all imaginable logical dimensions, except the one in which they contradict each other.

If contradiction occurs under these conditions then one statement is obviously wrong. This leads to a very important question that has a fundamental dimension of faith and belief: 'Is contradiction possible in religious texts?'

2. Contradiction between texts

An important aspect of faith is that we believe that contradiction, as between true and false, cannot apply to religious texts, whether they are in God's book or the statements of His messenger (peace be upon him). The entire text of the Qur'ān is available to us and it is absolutely clear that it admits no contradiction whatsoever. God says: '*Will they not, then, try to understand the Qur'ān? Had it issued from any but God, they would surely have found in it many an inner contradiction*.' (4: 82) According to Qatādah, 'What God says does not vary; it is the truth that admits no falsehood. It is people's words that vary.'[14] Al-Shāṭibī said: 'As for the possibility that there may be mutually exclusive proofs, if this means apparent contradiction in scholars' views, not an internal or intrinsic one, then this is possible, but that does not permit contradiction between evidence required by Islamic law. If, on the other hand, what is meant

13. 'Alā' al-Dīn 'Abd al-'Azīz al-Bukhārī, *Kashf al-Asrār Sharḥ Uṣūl al-Bazdāwī*, vol. 3, pp. 76–7.
14. Al-Ṭabarī, *Tafsīr*, vol. 5, p. 113.

is internal contradiction, this is something that cannot be entertained by anyone who understands Islamic law.'[15]

God's Messenger (peace be upon him) is also infallible and immune from saying what is contradictory. 'Otherwise, this would lead to imposing what cannot be fulfilled. Were we to assume that two clear statements are contradictory, yet both are intended by the Legislator... this would mean an order of "do and do not do" being given to the same person in one way. That would be precisely giving an order that cannot be fulfilled.'[16] However, mutual exclusion may occur in the sense of contradictory narrations of the Hadith. This is undoubtedly what scholars like Ibn al-Subkī explain as a fault due to narrators.[17] In such cases, duality is inevitable. There is no problem in Islam if a narrator makes a mistake in their narration.

We will draw attention to two types of contradiction due to narrators. The first is that of a narrator making an unintended mistake or forgetting something, which can apply to any human being. In this case, the contradiction is of the internal type. The other type is when one or more of the narrators are unreliable. In this case, one of the two pieces of evidence is defective and cannot be acceptable. As such it is not discarded arbitrarily but on solid grounds.

Case 1: When the contradiction in the two narrations is internal

If two Hadiths are internally contradictory, which means that there is unity in time, place, application, force, action, totality, part and condition, and that the only difference

15. Al-Shāṭibī, *al-Muwāfaqāt*, vol. 4, p. 129.
16. Ibid., p. 121.
17. 'Alī ibn 'Abd al-Kāfī al-Subkī and Tāj al-Dīn al-Subkī, *al-Ibhāj Sharḥ al-Minhāj*, vol. 3, p. 218.

between them is in negation and confirmation, and if there is no possibility that one of them is true and the other false, as logicians say, then they should be balanced according to recognised criteria in order to discard one of them. Here are some examples:

Example 1: ‘Ā’ishah reports the Hadith concerning omens being applied to mounts, women and homes. She says an oath that the Prophet (peace be upon him) said: ‘People used to say in the Days of Ignorance that omens are specifically felt in a woman, a home and a mount.’ This Hadith is accepted in preference to the one narrated by Abū Hurayrah which suggests that the Prophet himself said that omens are in these three. The preference is based on grounds of her memory, knowledge and her quotation of a Qur’ānic verse in support: ‘*No event takes place, either on earth or in yourselves, that is not recorded in a decree before We bring it into being*.’ (57: 22) Meticulous scholars say:

> What is reported from her by way of attributing the words to the people of the days prior to Islam is preferable, because she has retained things she learnt from the Prophet that others did not, particularly because good omens have been reported to be of these three types. Mu‘āwiyah ibn Ḥākim reports from his uncle Makhmar ibn Mu‘āwiyah that he said: ‘I heard God’s Messenger (peace be upon him) say: “No bad omens are valid. Good omens may be in a woman, a home and a mount.”’[18]

---

18. Yūsuf ibn Mūsā al-Ḥanafī, *Mu‘taṣar al-Mukhtaṣar*, vol. 2, p. 207. I researched this Hadith and I found it in largely similar versions in al-Tirmidhī, *Sunan*, ‘Book of Manners’; Ibn Mājah, *Sunan*, ‘Book of Marriage’; al-Ṭabarānī, *Musnad al-Shāmiyyīn*, and also in al-Ṭabarānī’s *al-Mu‘jam al-Kabīr* and *al-Mu‘jam al-Awsaṭ*, and al-Shaybānī’s *al-Āḥād wa al-Mathānī*. These have different chains of transmission, all of which converge on Ismā‘īl ibn ‘Ayyāsh. I could not find a specific grading of this Hadith, and so I examined

This is not contradicted by Ibn al-Jawzī's comment on 'Ā'ishah's report that 'it rejects a Hadith whose reporters are all reliable'.[19] Her own report is a clear Hadith, and all its reporters are reliable. I am amazed at Abū Bakr Ibn al-'Arabī's harshness in describing her statement on this matter as 'worthless'.[20] A scholar of his high calibre may not say such words against his mother, the Mother of the Believers. This example clearly indicates the influence of theological schools, and indeed male cultural prejudice, on the preferences and choices of some eminent scholars.

Example 2: The narration of Maymūnah, the Mother of the Believers: 'God's Messenger (peace be upon him) married me when we both were released from consecration (the state of *iḥrām*)', is given preference over Ibn 'Abbās's narration in which he mentions that 'he married her while he was in consecration'. Scholars give more weight to her narration because 'She was the one most involved. She was the one being married and she was more aware of the time when her marriage contract was made'.[21]

---

its reporters. These are: Ismā'īl ibn 'Ayyāsh: Imam Aḥmad says that his reporting from Syrian scholars is good. Yaḥyā ibn Ma'īn said: he is acceptable when reporting from Syrians. 'Alī ibn al-Madīnī, Ibn Abī Shaybah and 'Amr ibn al-Fallās grade him as reliable in reporting from Syrian scholars, but not from others. Sulaymān ibn Sulaym, a Syrian scholar, and Yaḥyā ibn Jābir are graded as reliable by Yaḥyā ibn Ma'īn, Abū Ḥātim al-Rāzī and others. Scholars differ as to whether Mu'āwiyah ibn Ḥākim was a Companion of the Prophet or not, but he is reliable. His uncle Makhmar was a Companion. As such, the Hadith is reported by reliable narrators and confirms 'Ā'ishah's narration.

19. Usāmah Khayyāṭ, *Mukhtalaf al-Ḥadīth Bayn al-Muḥaddithīn wa al-Uṣūliyyīn al-Fuqahā'*, p. 148.
20. Abū Bakr Muḥammad ibn 'Abd Allāh Ibn al-'Arabī, *'Aridat al-Ahwadhī*, vol. 10, pp. 264–5.
21. Badrān Abū al-'Aynayn Badrān, *Adillat al-Tashrī' al-Muta'āriḍah wa Wujūh al-Tarjīḥ Baynahā*, p. 131.

Example 3: Sufyān al-Thawrī and Abū Mu'āwiyah report from Suhayl from his father from Abū Hurayrah that God's Messenger (peace be upon him) said: 'If you see a funeral, stand up. Whoever follows it must not sit down until [the deceased] has been placed...' Abū Mu'āwiyah said, 'in the grave', while Sufyān said, 'in the ground'. Sufyān's narration is given preference because he had a better memory. Commenting on the two narrations, Abū Dāwūd said: 'Sufyān al-Thawrī is more accurate than Abū Mu'āwiyah.'[22] This is also the view of al-Bukhārī.[23]

Example 4: 'Ā'ishah's narration that the Prophet did not perform the *'umrah* in the month of Rajab is preferred to Ibn 'Umar's narration that he did. This preference is made on the grounds of 'Ā'ishah's perfect memorisation and her knowledge, as well as giving preference to narration by a larger number of people. Her report is confirmed by Anas's report. Ibn al-Jawzī said in his *al-Mushkil*: 'The fact that Ibn 'Umar did not reply [that is, after 'Ā'ishah had rejected his report] suggests one of two situations: either he started to doubt and remained silent, or he remembered what he had forgotten and kept silent. His silence means his agreement to what she had said. 'Ā'ishah reports this very accurately. Anas narrated: "God's Messenger (peace be upon him) performed *'umrah* four times, all of them in the month of Dhū al-Qa'dah". This Hadith clearly indicates that 'Ā'ishah was clear in her memorisation and that she was endowed with a high degree of understanding'.[24] May God reward Ibn al-Jawzī well for his perfect manners and his fair judgement.

22. Sulaymān ibn al-Ash'ath Abū Dāwūd, *Sunan Abī Dāwūd*, vol. 3, p. 200.
23. Al-Bukhārī, *Ṣaḥīḥ*.
24. Al-Suyūṭī, *'Ayn al-Iṣābah fī Istidrāk 'Ā'ishah 'alā al-Ṣaḥābah*, pp. 56–7.

Example 5: A Hadith describes the case of Barīrah[25] and her husband. Al-Qasim ibn Muḥammad narrated the story, mentioning that her husband was a slave. This was also narrated by 'Urwah, Mujāhid and 'Amrah bint 'Abd al-Raḥmān, with all these reporting from 'Ā'ishah. However, the same story as narrated by al-Aswad ibn Yazīd states that Mughīth was a free man, not a slave. Scholars give preference to al-Qāsim's report on the grounds that it is confirmed by other narrators, while al-Aswad's report is not. This is a case of preferring a report by a larger number of narrators. It is also preferred on the grounds of its being by a reporter seeing and listening to 'Ā'ishah, while al-Aswad's narration was based on listening from behind a screen. Both al-Qāsim and 'Urwah were 'Ā'ishah's nephews and they could see her in her home. Al-Qāsim's father was 'Ā'ishah's brother and 'Urwah's mother was her sister. Moreover, 'Amrah was brought up by 'Ā'ishah. Al-Aswad, on the other hand, could only listen to her when she was behind a screen.[26]

Example 6: The Hadith related by al-Bukhārī on Anas's authority stating that the Prophet offered his hajj pilgrimage in combination with the *'umrah* is preferred to Ibn 'Umar's

25. Barīrah, a slave woman, was married to Mughīth. She was set free and because her husband was a slave her marriage was then dissolved. Mughīth loved her and tried to keep the marriage. The Prophet (peace be upon him) suggested to her that she might do well to keep it. She asked whether he was giving her an order. The Prophet told her that he was not, but was speaking on Mughīth's behalf. She refused, and the Prophet did not put any pressure on her.

26. Nāfidh Ḥusayn Ḥammād, *Mukhtalaf al-Ḥadīth Bayn al-Fuqahā' wa al-Muḥaddithīn*, p. 258. I have cited this example only in the context of Hadiths mentioned by *fiqh* scholars in the context of contradiction. Today it has no practical application since the Universal Declaration of Human Rights ended slavery, which was signed by all Muslim countries. The Declaration is fully consistent with Islamic law, which makes the freedom of all people one of its main goals.

narration, also related by al-Bukhārī, that the Prophet (peace be upon him) offered his pilgrimage in the *ifrad* way, which does not include the *'umrah*. The preference here is made on the grounds that a narration agreed by all reporters is stronger than one which is the subject of disagreement. Anas's narration is consistent, without any disagreement, even though it is narrated by no fewer than sixteen reporters.[27] By contrast, al-Bukhārī gives another narration by Ibn 'Umar, which is authentic in as far as the chain of transmission is concerned, but different from the one quoted above. This one says: 'God's Messenger (peace be upon him) offered his farewell hajj the *tamattu'* way (with *'umrah* before the hajj)'. The argument that Anas was young at the time of the Prophet's hajj is discounted, because he was at least twenty years of age at the time.[28]

Example 7: Al-Tirmidhī relates a Hadith narrated by Samurah ibn Jundab that the Prophet read the Qur'ān silently during his prayer at the time of a solar eclipse. This is preferred to 'Ā'ishah's narration that he recited it aloud. The prayer during a solar eclipse was offered by the Prophet only once. The preference is made on the grounds that an agreed narration is preferable to one which is subject to disagreement. Abū Dāwūd enters a Hadith narrated by 'Ā'ishah: 'She guessed what the Prophet read in his prayer at the eclipse time, and she thought that he read surah 2, The Cow'. This clearly indicates that he did not recite the Qur'ān but read silently. This preference is confirmed by another narrator. Both al-Bukhārī and Muslim relate a Hadith narrated by Ibn 'Abbās that 'The Prophet stood up for a long time, close to [the time needed for] reading surah 2, The Cow'. This also suggests that he did not recite it aloud.

27. Al-Sawsawah, *Minhāj al-Tawfīq wa al-Tarjīḥ*, p. 379.
28. Ibid., p. 379.

In all these cases we realise that a mistake or an inaccuracy may have occurred, even in narrations by reliable and meticulous reporters. It is always a case of either one thing or the other being correct. Either bad omens may be in a woman, a house and a mount, or the rule is that there are no bad omens, only that people used to say this in pre-Islamic days. Both cannot be true. The Prophet's marriage to Maymūnah either took place while they were in the state of consecration or after they had released themselves from it. Either the Prophet (peace be upon him) performed *'umrah* in Rajab or he did not. Either Barīrah's husband was a slave or he was a free man. The Prophet's farewell pilgrimage was either in the *tamattu'* or the *ifrād* way. He either recited the Qur'ān aloud during the eclipse prayer or read it silently, as he offered this prayer only once.

Case 2: One of the two pieces of evidence is defective and cannot be acceptable

If a Hadith scholar finds that one of the two narrations is weak or defective in a way that makes it unacceptable, while the other is authentic, he must adopt the authentic or stronger narration. He must discard the other, giving it no consideration as a piece of evidence, as the Ḥanafī school maintains. The following examples illustrate this rule.

Example 1: Ibn 'Abd al-Barr rejects all fatwas based on [forbidding] disparity in marriage, because the Hadiths speaking about it are very poor in authenticity, while an authentic Hadith gives a general rule: 'If a man whose level of faith and manners are acceptable comes to you with a proposal of marriage, then accept his proposal'. Ibn 'Abd al-Barr wrote:

It is mentioned that the Prophet said: 'Marry [your women] to men of equal status, and beware of black people, because they are a disfigured creation'. This Hadith is rejected (*munkar*), false and has no basis. It is narrated by Dāwūd ibn al-Mujbir from Abū Umayyah ibn Ya'lā al-Thaqafī from Hishām ibn 'Urwah from his father from 'Ā'ishah. Both Dāwūd and Abū Umayyah are rejected as unreliable. Hence the Hadith is uncorroborated and lacks authenticity. The same ruling applies to a narration by Mubashshir from al-Ḥajjāj ibn Arta'ah from Jābir that the Prophet said: 'Do not marry women except to those who are of equal status'. It is very poor in authenticity, without foundation and not acceptable as evidence. Similarly a narration by Baqiyyah from Zur'ah from 'Imrān ibn al-Faḍl from Nāfi' from Ibn 'Umar from the Prophet is uncorroborated and fabricated. It says: 'Arabs are of equal status between themselves, a tribe to a tribe, a clan to a clan, one man to another, except for a weaver and one who administers cupping'. The same is also reported from Ibn Jurayj from Ibn Abī Malikah from Ibn 'Umar. Again, it cannot be true from Ibn Jurayj, but God knows best. The Prophet said: 'If a man whose level of faith and manners are acceptable comes to you with a proposal of marriage, then accept his proposal. Unless you do that, there will be oppression on earth and much corruption.' He did not specify an Arab or a freed slave. Taking it in its general meaning is certainly better.[29]

Example 2: Imam al-Nawawī gives a ruling that women may follow funeral processions, because he ruled that the Hadith related by Ibn Mājah in the 'Book of Funerals' is lacking in authenticity. The Hadith meant here is the one that tells women who followed a funeral: 'Go back bearing a burden, earning no reward'. Al-Nawawī comments: 'The

29. Yūsuf ibn 'Abd Allāh Ibn 'Abd al-Barr, *al-Tamhīd*, vol. 19, pp. 164–5.

chain of transmission of this Hadith is weak'.[30] He contrasts this with the Hadith also narrated by Ibn Mājah in the same 'Book of Funerals' concerning a bereaved woman weeping: 'Leave her alone, 'Umar: the eye is tearful, the bereavement is real and the event is recent'. Ibn Ḥajar comments on this Hadith saying: 'Its narrators are all reliable'.[31]

Example 3: On the question of combining the punishments of cutting a thief's hand and the thief providing compensation for the stolen property, Ibn Rushd said: 'Scholars differ on whether the material punishment of compensation for the stolen property may be combined with cutting the thief's hand. A number of scholars say that both apply. This is the view of al-Shāfi'ī, Aḥmad, al-Layth, Abū Thawr and others. Other scholars say that the thief does not incur the material punishment unless the stolen property itself is found with him. Among the scholars subscribing to this view are Abū Ḥanīfah, [Sufyān] al-Thawrī and Ibn Abī Laylā. The basis of this second view is the Hadith narrated by 'Abd al-Raḥmān ibn 'Awf quoting the Prophet: 'A thief does not incur the material punishment if the mandatory one is inflicted on him'.[32] Thus, Ibn Rushd makes the fact that this Hadith lacks in authenticity the basis for preferring the other view.

Example 4: Ibn Taymiyyah states a fatwa that a woman may recite the Qur'ān when she is menstruating. The basis of this fatwa is that he gives preference to authentic narrations about the women Companions of the Prophet over a narration that forbids women who are menstruating to recite the Qur'ān, because it lacks authenticity. He said:

---

30. Yaḥyā al-Nawawī, *al-Majmū'*, vol. 5, p. 237.
31. Ibn Ḥajar, *Fatḥ al-Bārī*, vol. 3, p. 173.
32. Muḥammad ibn Aḥmad Ibn Rushd, *Bidāyat al-Mujtahid wa Nihāyat al-Muqtaṣid*, vol. 2, p. 338.

> As for a menstruating woman reciting the Qur'ān, the Hadith reported by Ismā'īl ibn 'Ayyāsh from Mūsā ibn 'Uqbah from Nāfi' from Ibn 'Umar is not confirmed to be authentic. This Hadith says: 'A menstruating woman or a man in the state of ceremonial impurity (*janābah*) may not recite any part of the Qur'ān'. It is related by Abū Dāwūd and others, but it is classified by expert Hadith scholars as lacking authenticity. Hadiths reported by Ismā'īl ibn 'Ayyāsh from Ḥijāzī scholars are all poor in authenticity, unlike what he reports from Syrian scholars.[33] No reliable narrator has reported this Hadith from Nāfi'. Needless to say, women used to be in menstruation during the Prophet's lifetime but he did not forbid them reciting the Qur'ān.[34]

Example 5: In his voluminous book *al-Majmū'*, al-Nawawī said concerning horse meat:

> The view of our [Shāfi'ī] school is that it is permissible to eat, not discouraged. This is the view of most scholars... However, Abū Ḥanīfah held that a person is at fault for eating it, but it is not considered forbidden. His argument is based... on the Hadith narrated by Ṣāliḥ ibn Yaḥyā ibn al-Miqdam from his father from his grandfather from Khālid ibn al-Walīd which says: 'God's Messenger (peace be upon him) prohibited eating the meat of horses, mules and any wild animal with cutting front teeth.' This is related by Abū Dāwūd, al-Nasā'ī and Ibn Mājah... The Hadith scholar Mūsā ibn Hārūn al-Ḥammāl said: 'This Hadith lacks authenticity.' Al-Bukhārī said: 'This Hadith is questionable.' Al-Bayhaqī said: 'This Hadith has a confused chain of transmission, and in addition to this confusion, it is contrary to Hadiths narrated by reliable scholars, meaning Hadiths stating the permissibility of eating horse meat.' Al-Khaṭṭābī said: 'Its chain of transmission is questionable. It

33. We quoted earlier the views of Hadith scholars confirming this.
34. Ibn Taymiyyah, *Kutub wa Rasā'il wa Fatāwā*, vol. 21, p. 461.

> includes "Ṣāliḥ ibn Yaḥyā ibn al-Miqdam from his father from his grandfather."' It is not known that these heard Hadiths from each other... Our scholars cite in evidence the Hadith narrated by Jābir stating: 'At the time of [the Battle of] Khaybar, God's Messenger (peace be upon him) prohibited eating the meat of domestic donkeys but permitted horse meat.' This Hadith is related by both al-Bukhārī and Muslim in their *Ṣaḥīḥ*s.[35]

This, then, is a case of giving preference to an authentic Hadith over a Hadith that lacks authenticity and is rejected by scrupulous scholars.

Example 6: Al-Jassās gives preference to the view that vegetables are liable for Zakat on the basis of the greater weight he gives to the Hadith that includes 'what is irrigated by rain', which is a general Hadith with a recurrent meaning. He considers as lacking in authenticity the Hadith that says: 'No Zakat is payable on vegetables'. Al-Jassās says:

> The Hadith narrated by Mu'ādh, Ibn 'Umar and Jābir quotes the Prophet as saying: 'What is irrigated by rainwater pays one-tenth and what is irrigated with labour pays half of one-tenth.' This is a report that was generally accepted and implemented by people, and as such it amounts to the grade of *mutawātir*, or recurrent. The fact that it speaks generally makes the Zakat due applicable to all types of produce. If an argument is made on the basis of the Hadith narrated by Ya'qūb ibn Shaybah: al-Ḥārith ibn Shihāb narrated from 'Aṭā' ibn al-Ṣā'ib from Mūsā ibn Ṭalḥah from his father that God's Messenger (peace be upon him) said: 'No Zakat is payable on vegetables', the answer is that Ya'qūb ibn Shaybah, who narrated this Hadith, said that it is uncorroborated . Yaḥyā ibn Ma'īn used to say that any Hadith narrated by al-Ḥārith ibn Shihāb lacks authenticity.

35. Al-Nawawī, *al-Majmū'*, vol. 9, p. 6.

However, a careful examination of such Hadiths that appear contradictory[36] shows that such narrations are rare and have little effect on *fiqh*. The large majority of the Hadiths related to contradictory rulings do not meet one or more of the conditions that must apply in any case of contradiction, such as being related to different times or places or any other condition. In such a case, the contradiction is considered to be 'superficial' and to exist only in the recipient's mind, not intrinsically in the Hadiths. The discipline that discusses cases of contradiction is called *Mukhtalaf al-Ḥadīth*. The two main sources on which contemporary research in this discipline, including this book, relies are those by Imam al-Shāfi'ī and Imam Ibn Qutaybah.[37]

3. Ways of dealing with superficial contradiction

Superficial contradiction is defined as the case of 'two Hadiths that give seemingly contradictory meanings'.[38] 'What appears to us as contradiction, even if it is not really so, is what we allow ourselves to call contradiction.'[39] Scholars have established certain methods of dealing with these superficially contradictory Hadiths, comprising a series of well-defined stages: reconciliation, abrogation, preference, no-verdict, mutual negation and choice.

36. See, for example, the books by 'Abd Allāh Ibn Ḥazm, Qatādah, al-Karmī, and al-Nahhās, all entitled *al-Nāsikh wal Mansūkh*; Ibn al-Barazī, *Nāsikh al-Qur'ān wa Mansūkhuh*; Badrān, *Adillat al-Tashrī' al-Muta'āriḍah*; Ḥammād, *Mukhtalaf al-Ḥadīth*; Khayyāṭ, *Mukhtalaf al-Ḥadīth*; al-Sawsawah, *Minhāj al-Tawfīq wa al-Tarjīḥ*.
37. 'Abd Allāh ibn Muslim Ibn Qutaybah, *Ta'wīl Mukhtalaf al-Ḥadīth*; al-Shāfi'ī, *Ikhtilāf al-Ḥadīth*.
38. Al-Suyūṭī, *Tadrīb al-Rāwī*, vol. 2, p. 192.
39. Zayd, *al-Naskh fī al-Qur'ān al-Karīm*, vol. 1, p. 169.

Reconciliation is a method that looks for the logical difference that has led to the contradiction, such as different circumstances, people, times, and so on. Then the two are explained in the light of this logical difference.

Abrogation looks into the dates of the two Hadiths so as to adopt the later one as abrogating the earlier, which is then discarded. By abrogation, a Hadith is considered as cancelled and may not be implemented. We shall presently define and discuss abrogation, as it is the main topic of this book.

The preference method looks for the more authentic and accurate report in order to give it preference over the other, which is considered 'unpreferred'. In determining such preference, various factors are taken into consideration, such as the status of each reporter, the way and the time the narration was made, and its text,[40] as we have already discussed.

The no-verdict method allows scholars to admit inability to resolve the contradiction. They will then stop giving any rulings on the basis of either piece of evidence until they find a reason that enables them to reconcile the pieces of evidence, or determine preference or abrogation.[41]

Mutual negation is a method that drops both contradictory rulings 'because enforcing either one is in no way better than enforcing the other'.[42] Some scholars of legal theory express this as: 'Owing to their contradiction, they cancelled each other.'[43]

---

40. Badrān, *Adillat al-Tashrī' al-Muta'āriḍah*, p. 118.
41. Ḥammād, *Mukhtalaf al-Ḥadīth*, p. 127.
42. Al-Bukhārī, *Kashf al-Asrār*, vol. 3, p. 78.
43. Ḥammād, *Mukhtalaf al-Ḥadīth*, p. 127.

The choice method allows the scholar to give rulings using one Hadith at one time and the other at another time.[44]

As for the order of applying these methods, we find here a highly complex difference between scholars.[45] However, it appears to me from studying cases of contradiction that the methods of no-verdict, mutual negation and choice are very rarely used, since theoretically and practically, these have always come after the methods of reconciliation, abrogation and preference.

Some researchers consider that the methods of no-verdict and mutual negation 'are merely theoretical and have no practical effect'.[46] Imam al-Ḥaramayn al-Juwaynī considers them as 'mere assumptions'.[47] Al-Shāṭibī concludes that 'there are no two pieces of evidence that are mutually contradictory in a way that has caused Muslims to abstain by consensus from giving a ruling on their basis'.[48] However, it appears to me that adopting the attitude of 'no-verdict' is valid for individual scholars. It is the Prophet's Sunnah that a person who is unsure should say, 'I do not know'. Al-Bukhārī includes in his *Ṣaḥīḥ* a chapter entitled 'What the Prophet was asked about of questions regarding which he had no revelation and he said: "I do not know"'.[49] As for choice, it is reported that eminent scholars adopted it occasionally, giving verdicts that applied both Hadiths at different times. Ibn Kathīr described this as a 'bold' attitude.[50]

44. Ibid.
45. See, for example, Ḥammād, *Mukhtalaf al-Ḥadīth*; Khayyāṭ, *Mukhtalaf al-Ḥadīth*; al-Sawsawah, *Minhāj al-Tawfīq wa al-Tarjīḥ*.
46. Al-Sawsawah, *Minhāj al-Tawfīq wa al-Tarjīḥ*, p. 122.
47. Al-Juwaynī, *al-Burhān fī Uṣūl al-Fiqh*, vol. 2, p. 183.
48. Al-Shāṭibī, *al-Muwāfaqāt*, vol. 4, p. 294.
49. Al-Bukhārī, *Ṣaḥīḥ*, vol. 6, p. 2666.
50. Ibn Kathīr, *Ikhtiṣār 'Ulūm al-Ḥadīth*, p. 175.

It appears to me that this method involves some way of reconciliation. A *muftī* who gives a ruling according to one narration at one time and a different ruling according to the other narration at another time appears to choose what is more suitable to the case in question and what is closer to the objectives of Islamic law. This is one way of operating both texts. Therefore, we shall consider that the essential methods of dealing with cases of superficial contradiction are reconciliation, preference and abrogation. My study of cases of contradiction leads me to conclude that scholars (may God bestow mercy on them all) used abrogation more frequently than other methods. Hence, abrogation acquires special importance.

Chapter Three

Abrogation: Definitions and Uses

1. Linguistic and technical definitions

LINGUISTICALLY SPEAKING, *naskh*, or abrogation, means removal, as in 'the wind removed all traces'. It is also used to denote copying something, as in 'I have copied the book', meaning that I have written down all its contents, without removing it.[1]

In Islamic terminology, *naskh* appears to be used to denote different things, such as limited application, exception, interpretation of an earlier text with a later one, and cancelling an earlier ruling indicated by an earlier text with a later one.

1. Muḥammad ibn Abī Bakr al-Rāzī, *Mukhtar al-Ṣiḥāḥ*; also, Ibrāhīm ibn 'Alī al-Shīrāzī, *al-Luma' fī Uṣūl al-Fiqh*, vol. 1, p. 55.

2. The limitation, exception or interpretation of an earlier text by a later one

Limitation, exception and interpretation were commonly the meanings intended by the Prophet's Companions when they used the term *naskh*. As we have noted, their usage of this term did not mean practical cancellation of texts or annulment of rulings. It was purely a linguistic usage, which is perfectly appropriate. Here are some examples:

Example 1: In his *Sunan*, Abū Dāwūd relates that Ibn 'Abbās said: 'God said: "*As for the poets, only those who are lost in error follow them*." (26: 224) He then abrogated that making the following exception: "*Excepted for those who believe, and do righteous deeds, and remember God often*."'[2] (26: 227) Here abrogation is used in the sense of making an exception.

Example 2: Al-Nasā'ī relates: 'About the verse in surah 16, al-Naḥl: "*As for anyone who denies God after having accepted the faith – not one who does so under duress, while his heart remains true to his faith, but anyone who willingly opens his heart to unbelief: – upon all such falls God's wrath, and theirs will be a tremendous punishment*" (16: 106) Ibn 'Abbās said, He then abrogated that by making an exception: "*But then, your Lord [grants forgiveness] to those who forsake their homes after enduring trials and persecution, and strive hard [in God's cause] and remain patient in adversity. After this, your Lord is certainly much-forgiving, ever merciful*."'[3] (16: 110) Again this is a case of using abrogation in the sense of an exception.

---

2. Abū Dāwūd, *Sunan*, 'Book of Manners', chapter on poetry.
3. Aḥmad ibn Shu'ayb al-Nasā'ī, *al-Sunan al-Kubrā*, 'Book of Forbidding Bloodshed', chapter on repentance by apostates.

Example 3: Abū Dāwūd relates that Ibn 'Abbās said: The verses: '*If you do not go forth to fight [in God's cause], He will punish you severely and replace you by other people*' (9: 39) and '*It does not behove the people of Madīnah and the desert Arabs who live around them to hold back from following God's Messenger, or to care for themselves more than for him; for, whenever they endure thirst, stress, or hunger for the sake of God, or take any step which would irritate the unbelievers, or inflict any loss on the enemy, a good deed is recorded in their favour. God does not suffer the reward of those who do good to be lost. And whenever they spend anything for the sake of God, be it little or much, or traverse a valley, it is recorded for them, so that God will give them the best reward for what they do.*' (9: 120–1) These were all abrogated by the following verse: '*It is not desirable that all the believers should go out to fight. From every section of them some should go forth, so that they may acquire a deeper knowledge of the faith and warn their people when they return to them, so that they may take heed.*' (9: 122)

Abrogation in this sense means explanation and providing details.

Example 4: Ibn Mājah relates that Abū Sa'īd al-Khudrī recited verses 282 and 283 of surah 2, which outline rulings on borrowing. When he recited the statement: '*If you trust one another, let him who is trusted fulfil his trust, and let him fear God, his Lord*' (2: 283), he said that this statement abrogated what came before it. This second verse addresses a special case of travel when both lender and borrower complete their transaction on the basis of mutual trust.

In all these examples, it is clear that abrogation does not mean cancellation or removal or annulment of a meaning, a text or a ruling stated in what is abrogated, as may be linguistically implied. It means limitation, explanation or exception.

3. Abrogation as meaning final annulment of a religious ruling

When we consider the use of abrogation to mean the annulment of religious rulings, we find that books of legal theory agree on a part of the definition. This part says: 'Abrogation is the cancellation of a religious ruling by a later text providing evidence.'[4] Cancellation in this sense is meant to be final so as to exclude any possibility of implementing the abrogated ruling. Scholars also agree on their rejection of the Jews' claim that no abrogation takes place, allegedly basing this claim on negating that something new occurs to God. This is an aspect of their rejection that the Jewish law was abrogated by the Prophet Muḥammad's message.[5]

There are differences over parts of the definition of abrogation which may be considered linguistic differences, because they are not concerned with any practical *fiqh* issues, such as: Is the abrogating ruling an explanation or substitution of the abrogated one? Does the abrogating ruling put an end to the abrogated one, in the sense that without the new ruling the abrogated one would have remained in

---

4. Al-Shāfi'ī, *al-Risālah*, p. 108; al-Juwaynī, *al-Burhān fī Uṣūl al-Fiqh*, vol. 2, p. 843; al-Amidī, *al-Aḥkām*, vol. 3, p. 127; Ibn Ḥazm, *al-Iḥkām fī Uṣūl al-Aḥkām*, vol. 7, p. 380; al-Shawkānī, *Irshād al-Fuḥūl ilā Taḥqīq al-Ḥaqq min 'Ilm al-Uṣūl*, vol. 1, p. 244; Ibn Taymiyyah, *al-Muswaddah fī Uṣūl al-Fiqh*, vol. 1, p. 178; al-Ghazālī, *al-Mustaṣfā*, vol. 1, p. 86; Muḥammad al-Barakātī, *Qawā'id al-Fiqh*, vol. 1, p. 212; al-Shīrāzī, *al-Luma' fī Uṣūl al-Fiqh*, vol. 1, p. 55.
5. Ibn Taymiyyah, *al-Muswaddah fī Uṣūl al-Fiqh*, vol. 1, p. 176; al-Juwaynī, *al-Burhān fī Uṣūl al-Fiqh*, vol. 2, p. 842; 'Abd al-'Aẓīm al-Zurqānī, *Manāhil al-'Irfān*, vol. 2, p. 163.

force? Did the abrogated ruling have a limited duration of applicability, regardless of the abrogating ruling? Can abrogation apply to a text the wording of which indicates that its ruling is permanent? Does abrogation apply to information and orders, or to orders only? Is it possible to abrogate a requirement before people are able to fulfil it?

However, abrogation in its agreed sense by *fiqh* scholars, which is the permanent annulment of a religious ruling by a later one, is our main concern here, because it is closely linked to both issues of contradiction between texts and changing rulings.

Chapter Four

A Critique of some Methodologies Confirming Abrogation

1. Is there any definitive evidence of the abrogation of any Qur'ānic verses?

THERE ARE some reports that claim that the wording of certain verses of the Qur'ān was abrogated after the verses had been written down. This claim is absolutely untrue. Indeed, it opens the door to raising doubts about the Book of God, which cannot be touched by any falsehood either openly or surreptitiously. Moreover, God, who revealed the Qur'ān, has guaranteed that it shall remain forever immune to any change or distortion. Hence, although some of these reports are entered in authentic Hadith collections, I do not find in them anything to suggest that there is any merit in considering the issue of abrogated wording.

This leaves us with verses containing 'abrogated rulings'. When we look for the words *naskh* (abrogation) and *tabdīl* (substitution) in God's book, we find them used on two occasions only. The first uses a derivation of *naskh*: '*Any revelation that We annul or consign to oblivion We replace with a better or similar one. Do you not know that God has power over all things?*' (2: 106) The other uses the verbal form of *tabdīl*: '*When We replace one verse by another – and God knows best what He reveals – they say: "You are but a fabricator." Indeed most of them have no knowledge.*' (16: 101)

Most commentators on the Qur'ān consider that the second verse (that is, the verse from surah 16) speaks about the annulment of earlier codes of law. Explaining it, al-Qurṭubī says: 'It means replacing an earlier code of law by a new one.' Al-Ṭabarī quotes Mujāhid: 'It means to abrogate, replace, remove and put another in its place.' According to Qatādah the two above-quoted verses are similar. About the reason for its revelation al-Nasafī says: 'They used to say that Muḥammad made fun of his Companions, giving them an order to do something today and forbidding them to do it tomorrow, giving them what is easier. They were wrong, as he used to replace what was more difficult by an easier one, and replace what was easy by a more difficult one. Most of them have no knowledge of the wisdom behind it.'Shaykh Muḥammad al-Ghazālī (may God bestow mercy on him) objected to this explanation. He noted that 'surah 16, The Bees, was revealed in Makkah. No earlier revelation was annulled and replaced by another that was more difficult or easy... Moreover, there is no reference in the Prophet's life history to any objection by the unbelievers or any question by believers concerning abrogation. Indeed, throughout the life of the first Islamic society, no verse revealed to state that something was permissible was ever followed by another verse revealing its prohibition.' He adds: 'We can categorically say that none of the unbelievers in Makkah entertained any thought of what some commentators consider to be the reason for the revelation of this verse.

Indeed, this is a case of explaining verses according to the views of scholars of *fiqh* and theology. It thus charges the Qur'ān with meanings that are different from those of its words and verses. The correct explanation of this verse maintains that the unbelievers were not convinced that the Qur'ān itself was a miracle confirming Muḥammad's prophethood. They looked for a supernatural event… God, the Exalted and Mighty, responded to them that this miracle, the Qur'ān, was better for people and a much longer lasting reason for accepting and confirming the faith than any other sign.'[1]

Shaykh al-Ghazālī's view appears to me an apt interpretation of the verse, consistent with its time of revelation in Makkah and what is known of the Prophet's life history. It is also consistent with the subject matter of the surah as it refutes the objections raised by the unbelievers and the doubts they reiterated about the Islamic message.

The verse mentioning abrogation is: '*Any revelation that We annul or consign to oblivion We replace with a better or similar one. Do you not know that God has power over all things?*' (2: 106) Most commentators express the view that it speaks of the annulment of rulings stated in some verses, or causing some verses to be forgotten. This I find wholly unacceptable, either with regard to wording, as mentioned above, or ruling, as we will discuss below. To me, the verse speaks about the annulment of some rulings in earlier laws and the replacement of them with new rulings included in Islamic law.

However, in his comments on this verse, al-Ṭabarī said: 'It means making forbidden what was permissible and making what was forbidden lawful.'[2] Referring to the

1. Muḥammad al-Ghazālī, *Naẓarāt fī al-Qur'ān*, pp. 202–4.
2. Al-Ṭabarī, *Tafsīr*.

reason for the revelation of this verse, al-Qurṭubī said: 'The Jews envied the fact that Muslims faced the Ka'bah in their prayer, and they used this as material to slander Islam. They said that Muḥammad gave one order to his Companions one day then he forbade them to do it. This confirms that the Qur'ān was of his own invention and, as such, it is self-contradictory. Therefore, God revealed the verses: "When We replace one verse by another," and also "Any revelation We annul or consign to oblivion."'[3]

The first verse cited by al-Qurṭubī here is the same verse in surah 16, saying '*When We replace one verse by another*,' but it was revealed in Makkah where there were no Jews to criticise Islam and nothing was known yet about the change of the direction Muslims face when they pray.[4] However, al-Qurṭubī chose to link this verse to the abrogation of rulings, and severely criticised anyone who did not share this view of abrogation: 'Knowledge of this aspect is necessary and its usefulness is great. Scholars cannot dispense with this knowledge, and it is only denied by people who are ignorant and stupid. For it relates to the latest legislation outlining rulings and the knowledge of what is permissible and what is forbidden'.[5] Shaykh Muḥammad al-Ghazālī, who was neither ignorant nor stupid, took a different line of reasoning while interpreting this verse. He comments: 'It severs the verse from what comes before it and what comes after it. Indeed, it makes it unrelated to the whole atmosphere of the surah, which starts to take issue with the people of earlier revelations and condemns their attitudes, referring to their stubborn rejection of the Prophet Muḥammad and his

3. Muḥammad ibn Aḥmad al-Qurṭubī, *Tafsīr*.
4. Muḥammad Maḥmūd Nadā, *al-Naskh fī al-Qur'ān Bayn al-Mu'ayyidīn wa al-Mu'āriḍīn*, p. 40.
5. Al-Qurṭubī, *Tafsīr*, vol. 2, p. 61.

message. They wanted him to produce supernatural miracles of the type given to Jewish Prophets and familiar to them'.[6]

Shaykh al-Ghazālī's view is shared by many contemporary scholars. Imam Muḥammad 'Abduh interprets the verse[7] and says:

> The correct meaning that fits the context of the surah to its end is that the word *āyah* [which can mean a sign or a Qur'ānic verse] in this instance refers to the proofs God gives to Prophets to confirm their prophethood. Thus 'Any revelation We annul' means in the first place 'A sign We give in confirmation of anyone's prophethood. We may later annul it, without using it to support another Prophet, or We may consign it to oblivion so that people completely forget it. We have unrestricted ability and control of the universe. So We bring instead something better and more convincing in confirming prophethood, or at least something of equal effect.' ... What makes the meaning clearer is that God says shortly afterwards: '*Do you wish to ask of the Messenger who has been sent to you the same as was formerly asked of Moses?*'[8] (2: 108)

It should be mentioned that al-Rāzī quotes Abū Muslim al-Aṣfahānī expressing a similar interpretation, and includes this with several other interpretations of this verse he quotes. These include: 'The annulled revelations refer to the laws included in the older revelations (that is, the Torah and the Gospel), such as the Sabbath and facing east or west in prayer. God has annulled these and assigned to us other forms of worship. The Jews and the Christians used to say

6. Al-Ghazālī, *Nazarat fī al-Qur'ān*, p. 204.
7. Muḥammad 'Abduh, *Tafsīr al-Qur'ān al-Ḥakīm*, vol. 1, p. 418; quoted and supported by 'Alī Ḥasab Allāh, *Uṣūl al-Tashrī' al-Islāmī*, p. 355.
8. Al-Ghazālī, *Naẓarāt fī al-Qur'ān*, p. 204.

that they would not believe anyone except one who follows their own religions. God refutes their argument through this verse.'[9]

As quoted by al-Rāzī, Abū Muslim believes that abrogation is limited to the annulment of earlier messages and codes of law. Abrogation of Qur'ānic verses stating certain rulings, in the sense that such rulings become null and void, has not been proven. This seems to me to be the case. In his commentary on the Qur'ān, al-Rāzī favours this view and supports the ways Abū Muslim suggested to reconcile the verses detailing rulings some of which are claimed to be abrogated. Al-Rāzī quotes Abū Muslim's views on these as they occur in the Qur'ān.

On the basis of the comments we have mentioned, we may draw the following conclusions:

1. There is no specific and definitive evidence to suggest that anything in the Qur'ān refers to abrogation in the sense of the annulment of the rulings outlined in specific verses. This is clear from the differences in interpreting the texts that refer to 'abrogation'.
2. The interpretation that links such verses to the queries of the unbelievers in Makkah, or to forbidding something that was earlier ruled lawful, or changing the status of something from lawful to forbidden, or substituting something difficult with another that is easier, and so on, is a laboured interpretation. Besides, as Shaykh Muḥammad al-Ghazālī has said, none of the actual events recorded in the Prophet's life history suggest or confirm it.

9. Al-Rāzī, *Mafātīḥ al-Ghayb*, vol. 2, p. 626.

3. I feel that the more valid interpretation of the verse that says, '*Any revelation We annul or consign to oblivion*', is that of Abū Muslim, linking it to the annulment of the Jewish code of law. This understanding of the verse accepts the principle of abrogation of earlier rulings and is consistent with the overall context, which is the refutation of the argument made by the Jews at the time. Scholars stress that subject unity and context are important elements that need to be considered when explaining Qur'ānic verses.[10]

4. Even if this verse is correctly deemed to refer to the principle of abrogating certain verses or rulings of the Qur'ān, as maintained by the majority of scholars, it does not suggest that such abrogation actually took place with regard to a particular part of the Qur'ān. To claim this requires specific evidence. One cannot conclude that a particular verse or ruling of the Qur'ān is abrogated, in the sense of a definitive annulment, on the basis of personal opinion. It requires acceptable evidence and a well-defined methodology of consideration of this evidence in order to prove not only the annulment but also its finality. The next part of this chapter discusses the methods adopted by scholars to indicate abrogation on the basis of detailed evidence.

10. See various studies on the 'thematic interpretation of the Qur'ān', which have been on the increase in the past century. Here are some examples: Muḥammad 'Abduh, *Tafsīr al-Qur'ān al-Ḥakīm*; Bāqir al-Ṣadr, *Muqaddimāt fī al-Tafsīr al-Mawḍū'ī*; Ibn 'Āshūr, Introduction to *al-Taḥrīr wa al-Tanwīr*; Ḥasan al-Turābī, *al-Tafsīr al-Tawḥīdī*; Muḥammad 'Abd Allāh Drāz, *al-Nabā' al-'Aẓīm*, translated as *The Qur'ān: An Eternal Challenge*; Muḥammad al-Ghazālī, *Naḥwa Tafsīr Mawḍū'ī*, translated as *A Thematic Commentary on the Qur'ān*; and Yūsuf al-Qaradāwī, *Kayfa Nata'āmal ma' al-Qur'ān al-Karīm*; there are many others.

2. Contradiction as evidence for abrogation

Scholars of legal theory (*uṣūl al-fiqh*) define contradiction that leads to suggest abrogation as 'contradiction in the same matter', which means logical contradiction. Thus, these scholars make it a condition that two Hadiths must be contradictory and cannot be reconciled to enable a scholar to rule that one abrogates the other. Imam al-Shāfi'ī states a very important rule in this regard, even though he himself did not always apply it. He wrote:

> If two Hadiths are at clear variance, as in the variance between facing Jerusalem or facing the Ka'bah in prayer, then one of them abrogates and the other is abrogated. Whenever we have two Hadiths and both can be implemented together, they both should be implemented. Neither may stop the other.[11]

However, Abū Ḥāmid al-Ghazālī wrote: 'If two texts are mutually contradictory, the one that came later abrogates the earlier'.[12] Imam al-Juwaynī adds that the aim of claiming abrogation is 'to ensure that there is no contradiction in God's Word'.[13] Al-Zurqānī says about abrogation in his *Manāhil al-'Irfān*: 'Abrogation is a necessity that may only be invoked in cases of real contradiction, so as to prevent contradiction in the legislation of God, the Wise, the All-Knowing. His is a Book that admits no falsehood either openly or stealthily.'[14] My comment on all this is that God's book does not need our logic to prove that it is free of all falsehood and contradiction.

---

11. Al-Shāfi'ī, *Ikhtilāf al-Ḥadīth*, vol. 1, p. 487.
12. Al-Ghazālī, *al-Mustaṣfā*, vol. 1, p. 103.
13. Al-Juwaynī, *al-Burhān fī Uṣūl al-Fiqh*, vol. 2, p. 844.
14. Al-Zurqānī, *Manāhil al-'Irfān*, vol. 2, p. 128.

Anyone who studies sources of *fiqh* and Qur'ānic commentary will realise that the condition of logical contradiction is not met in most cases, or claims, of abrogation in the Qur'ān or in the Sunnah. These claims are made on the basis of superficial variance that some scholars clearly understood while others did not. The following examples show that there is no real contradiction in many cases in the Qur'ān where claims of abrogation have been made.

Example 1: God says: '*Believers, spend [for God's cause] out of that with which We have provided you before there comes a day when there will be no trading, or friendship or intercession. Truly, the unbelievers are the wrongdoers.*' (2: 254) He also says: '*[True believers] attend regularly to their prayers and spend in charity some of what We have provided them with.*' (8: 3) Both verses are claimed to have been abrogated by the verse that mentions the beneficiaries of Zakat: '*Charitable donations are only for the poor and the needy, and those who work in the administration of such donations, and those whose hearts are to be won over, for the freeing of people in bondage and debtors, and to further God's cause, and for the traveller in need. This is a duty ordained by God, and God is All-knowing, Wise.*' (9: 60) The claim of abrogation is made on the basis of contradiction assumed by some commentators. The fact is that 'there is no contradiction between them. The spending in the first two verses is understood to cover obligatory Zakat and voluntary charity, as well as what one spends on one's family and relatives, and so on. In this case the verse explaining Zakat is understood to mention a specific case of a general meaning'.[15]

15. Ibid., p. 183.

Example 2: The following verse is claimed to be abrogated: '*Believers! Fear God as you rightly should, and do not allow death to overtake you before you have surrendered yourselves truly to Him.*' (3: 102) Indeed, al-Suyūṭī said: 'No verse in surah 3, Āl 'Imrān, may be rightly claimed to be abrogated except this one.'[16] It is said that it is abrogated by the verse that says: '*Therefore, remain God-fearing as best as you can.*' (64: 16) Al-Zurqānī refutes this claim: 'It is not abrogated, because the fear of God required by the first verse is explained as "one should ensure to be right in one's mind and what it understands, and also one's stomach and what it contains, and to remember death and what comes after it. Undoubtedly, all this is within man's ability with God's help. Therefore, there is no contradiction between these two verses. Where there is no contradiction there can be no abrogation."'[17]

Example 3: God says to His messenger concerning disputes put to him by the Jews: '*Hence, if they come to you [for judgement], you may either judge between them or decline to interfere.*' (5: 42) It is claimed that this verse was abrogated by the later verse in the same surah: '*Hence, judge between them in accordance with what God has revealed, and do not follow their vain desires.*' (5: 49) The claim of abrogation does not stand. The latter verse complements the former, because the first of these two verses gives him a choice of either judging between them or declining to do so. However, the second verse tells him that if he chooses to judge between them he must judge in accordance with what God has revealed.[18]

16. Al-Suyūṭī, *al-Itqān fī 'Ulūm al-Qur'ān*, vol. 2, p. 161.
17. Al-Zurqānī, *Manāhil al-'Irfān*, vol. 2, p. 188.
18. Ibid., p. 189.

Example 4: God says concerning the prohibition of fighting in the sacred months: '*They ask you about fighting in the sacred month. Say, "Fighting in it is a grave offence, but to turn people away from God's path, to disbelieve in Him and in the Sacred Mosque, and to expel its people from it – [all this] is far more grave in God's sight.*"' (2: 217) Ibn Jarīr reports from 'Aṭā' ibn Maysarah that it was abrogated by the verse '*But fight against the idolaters all together as they fight against you all together.*' (9: 36) According to Abū Ja'far al-Nahhās, all scholars except 'Aṭā' agree that this constitutes abrogation.[19] They argue that 'the second verse gives general permission to the Muslim community to fight the unbelievers. Since the permission applies to people generally, it also applies to times generally'. It is also suggested that the first of these verses is abrogated by the verse that says: '*Slay the idolaters wherever you find them.*' (9: 5) 'As this statement applies to all places generally, it also applies to all times. Such is the view of the majority of scholars, but it is countered by the fact that the generality of people in Verse 9: 36 and the generality of places in 9: 5 do not necessarily mean a generality of times as well. Therefore, we see neither contradiction nor abrogation in this case.'[20] It should be noted that the claim of abrogation is based on indefinite logic and lacks accuracy.

Here are a few additional examples – and there are many more – from the Prophetic Sunnah which serve as evidence that claims of abrogation are wrong when they are made on the basis of superficial contradiction suggested by a scholar or a narrator or a commentator who might not have thought of a different way to reconcile such reports.

19. Ibid., p. 186.
20. Ibid.

Example 1: We have different views on the question of wiping over one's *khuffs*,[21] instead of washing one's feet when performing the ablution. There are reports from the Prophet concerning this and they appear to be superficially contradictory. Scholars express three different views, with some resorting to giving preference to certain reports, others claiming abrogation and still others leaning towards reconciling these reports. Al-Ḥasan al-Baṣrī and Imam Aḥmad adopt many such narrations, amounting to the grade of *tawātur*, which is the highest grade of authenticity.[22] They prefer these as they say that God's Messenger (peace be upon him) wiped over his *khuffs*. However, 'Alī ibn Abī Talib considered that the ruling allowing such wiping was abrogated. He said: 'God's Messenger wiped over his *khuffs* before the revelation of the verse in surah 5, The Repast [which includes the details of ablution], but did not do so after its revelation.'[23] What is strange is that Ibn 'Abbās, 'Ā'ishah and Abū Hurayrah agreed with this.[24] However, the majority of the Prophet's Companions and the overwhelming majority of scholars, in all generations, have considered that wiping over *khuffs* is valid as a concession, even though washing one's feet is preferable. They consider that if it was not practised by the Prophet in a certain period, that does not

---

21. *Khuffs* are soft footwear made of leather or cloth and are worn the way we wear socks these days. A person who performs the ablution may wipe over them with their hands instead of the normal requirement of washing one's feet up to one's ankles. There are certain well-known conditions that apply to this concession.
22. Al-Ḥasan counted seventy such reports, while Imam Aḥmad counted forty. Ibn Ḥajar considered that there are more than eighty. See al-Sawsawah, *Minhāj al-Tawfīq wa al-Tarjīḥ*, p. 401.
23. Related by Abū Khālid al-Wāsiṭī in *Musnad al-Imām Zayd*. See al-Sawsawah, *Minhāj al-Tawfīq wa al-Tarjīḥ*, p. 400.
24. Muḥammad ibn Ismā'īl al-Ṣan'ānī, *Subul al-Salām*, vol. 1, p. 58. See al-Sawsawah, *Minhāj*, p. 400.

mean that it is unacceptable.[25] What the Companions believed, which is the basis of the argument of most scholars, is that the Prophet always practised such wiping. We have one authentic report to this effect, related by al-Bukhārī on the authority of Jarīr ibn ʻAbd Allāh. The time of this report is later than the revelation of surah 5, as Jarīr, the narrator, was 'among the last [of the Companions] to accept Islam'. All this goes to show that the contradiction was not real, let alone an abrogation or annulment. It was an apparent contradiction in some of the Companions' minds.

Example 2: Some scholars consider that there is some contradiction in the reports speaking of tanning as a way of removing impurity from the hides of animals that die naturally. Some of them go further and state that this constitutes abrogation. This is explained by Ibn Rushd in his highly valuable book, *Bidāyat al-Mujtahid*:

> Scholars differ with regard to making use of the hides of dead animals. Some consider it perfectly permissible, whether the hides are tanned or not. Others take exactly the opposite view, making it forbidden even when tanned. A third group makes a difference between tanned and untanned hides. This third group considers tanning as a method of removing impurity. This is the view of al-Shāfiʻī and Abū Ḥanīfah... The reason for this difference is that there are contradictory reports on this question. A Hadith narrated by Maymūnah relates that the Prophet saw a dead animal. He commented to those with him: 'Would it

25. See, for example, al-Jassās, *Aḥkām al-Qur'ān*, vol. 3, p. 353; Ibn Kathīr, *Tafsīr*, vol. 2, p. 29; al-Qurṭubī, *Tafsīr*, vol. 6, p. 93; Ibn Qudāmah, *al-Mughnī*, vol. 1, p. 174; Ibn Taymiyyah, *Kutub wa Rasā'il wa Fatāwā*, vol. 21, p. 21; al-Ṣanʻānī, *Subul al-Salām*, vol. 1, p. 57.

> not be better for you to make use of its hide?'[26] Another Hadith narrated by Ibn 'Ukaym states that the Prophet dictated: 'You shall not make use of any part of a dead animal, even its hide or nerves.' This was one year before he passed away.[27] A confirmed Hadith on this issue is the one narrated by Ibn 'Abbās quoting the Prophet: 'When a hide is tanned, it has become cleansed.'[28] Owing to the difference between these Hadiths, scholars differed in their interpretation. Some opted for reconciling them according to Ibn 'Abbās's narration, differentiating between what is tanned and what is not regarding using them. Others chose the ruling of abrogation, opting for the Hadith narrated by Ibn 'Ukaym, because it states that it was 'one year before the Prophet passed away'.[29]

The preference for reconciling these reports is endorsed by Abū Dāwūd, who was the one who related Ibn 'Ukaym's narration. Abū Dāwūd comments on these Hadiths, dispelling their apparent contradiction: 'When hide has been tanned it is no longer called *īhāb*.'[30] Thus, he understands that the permission applies to what is tanned and the prohibition to what is not tanned, regardless of the

26. Muslim, *Ṣaḥīḥ*, vol. 1, p. 276. Ibn 'Abbās narrated: 'A maid of Maymūnah's was given a lamb as charity, but the lamb died. The Prophet passed by and said: "Would it not be better that you take its hide, have it tanned and make use of it?" They said: "It died naturally." He said: "What is forbidden is to eat it,"' as it was carrion.
27. Abū Dāwūd, *Sunan*, vol. 4, p. 67. 'Abd Allāh ibn 'Ukaym reported that God's Messenger (peace be upon him) sent to [the tribe of] Juhaynah, one month before he passed away – another report mentions one year (instead of one month). He said that they 'may not make use of any part of dead animals, including their hide and nerves'.
28. Muslim, *Ṣaḥīḥ*, vol. 1, p. 277.
29. Ibn Rushd, *Bidāyat al-Mujtahid*, vol. 1, p. 57.
30. *Ihab* is the word used by the Prophet in the Hadith narrated by Ibn 'Ukaym.

superficial contradiction between the different Hadiths and which was said earlier and which was said later. He saw no reason for making this a case of abrogation.[31]

On the basis of what we said earlier in defining contradiction, all the examples we have cited contain no contradiction of the type of facing two different directions in prayer at the same time. This is what Imam al-Shāfi'ī mentioned in his definition of contradiction. All these examples speak of texts that scholars considered to suggest superficial contradiction, but scholars of old or recent times who have understood such questions have been able to remove the resulting confusion. Therefore, the claims of abrogation in all the cited examples and similar ones are unacceptable because none of them meet the condition of true contradiction imposed by scholars of legal theory. Moreover, there is no evidence to support the basic claim of abrogation denoting annulment.

3. Abrogation on the basis of dates: are we required to adopt the latest?

The Companions were exemplary in their obedience and implementation of the Prophet's orders. God says: '*Whenever God and His Messenger have decided a matter, it is not for a believing man or woman to claim freedom of choice in that matter*.' (33: 36) Therefore, they used to follow the most recent of what was revealed of the Qur'ān and of the Prophet's orders. They also encouraged one another to do so. Al-Zuhrī said: 'They used to follow the most recent of the Prophet's orders, and they considered it as

31. Abū Dāwūd, *Sunan*, vol. 4, p. 67.

abrogating the earlier and as definitive.'[32] When the Islamic message was complete and the Prophet passed away, his Companions faced new questions and they differed on them. They referred to the Qur'ān and the Prophet's Sunnah, but they still found some matters in which following the most recent Qur'ānic revelations or Hadiths was problematic. Their views on these divided them into three groups:

The first group had heard one report, either the earlier or the later one. They adhered to what they had heard. This applied to the Prophet's Sunnah only, because the Qur'ān was known to them all.

The second group had heard both texts and implemented the later one when they heard it, considering the later verse or the Hadith as abrogating the earlier verse or Hadith. They did not allow the implementation of the earlier one in any way.

The third group also heard both texts and also implemented the later one when they heard it. However, they understood from the verses, or from the Prophet's words, or from the historical context of events, that there were differences between the two cases. Therefore, they endeavoured to implement both texts, each according to its relevant circumstances.

These differences between the Prophet's Companions had a great effect on the schools of *fiqh*, which is clearly seen in questions of detail. We find that some scholars give preference to one of different narrations that lead to contradictory results, even though all these narrations are

---

32. A comment by Ibn Shihāb al-Zuhrī on the question of travellers not fasting: Muslim, *Ṣaḥīḥ*, vol. 2, p. 789. A similar report is in al-Bayhaqī, *al-Sunan al-Kubrā*, vol. 4, p. 246. The same is reported in 'Abd ibn Ḥumayd's *Musnad*, and by Ibn 'Abbās, as well as many other books of Hadith.

confirmed to be authentic. We have already discussed this. Other scholars opt for abrogation, which entails the final annulment of the earlier text, adopting the later one when there is an indication of the dates of the two texts. For example, al-Sarakhsī said: 'Do you not see that when dates are known, no contradiction occurs in any way? The later text abrogates the earlier one.'[33] Yet by God's grace we find in each case a third group who succeed in finding a rule or a conclusion that reconciles the two authentic texts, making it possible to enforce both.

Here are some examples of *fiqh* questions that have been based on the inaccurate understanding of the abrogation of some verses of God's book. Yet scholars among the Prophet's Companions rectified such inaccuracies.

Example 1: Concerning the division of a deceased person's estate among his or her heirs, God says: '*When other kinsfolk, orphans and needy persons are present at the distribution of inheritance, give them something out of it, and speak to them in a kindly way.*' (4: 8) Some of the Prophet's Companions thought that this verse was abrogated by the verses that were revealed later defining the heirs and their shares of inheritance. Ibn 'Abbās comments on the above-mentioned verse: 'Some people claim that this verse has been abrogated. By God, it is not; but this is a case of people taking it lightly. It speaks of two types: one inherits, and this type is the one given something of the estate. The other does not inherit; this is the one to whom kind words are to be spoken.'[34] Therefore, 'when Ibn 'Abbās was in charge, he complied (by giving something)'.[35] Ibn 'Abbās's understanding disproves the claim of abrogation on the basis

33. Al-Sarakhsī, *Uṣūl al-Sarakhsī*, vol. 2, p. 112.
34. Ibn Ḥajar, *Fatḥ al-Bārī*, vol. 8, p. 242.
35. Ibid. See also al-Rāzī, *Mukhtār al-Ṣiḥāḥ*, vol. 1, p. 103.

of assumed contradiction. It allows the implementation of both verses, each in its own sphere, regardless of which was revealed earlier and which later.

Example 2: God revealed: '*To God belongs all that is in the heavens and the earth. Whether you make known what is in your minds or conceal it, God will bring you to account for it. He will then forgive whom He wills and punish whom He wills. God has power over all things.*' (2: 284) He later revealed: '*God does not charge a soul with more than it can bear. In its favour shall be whatever (good) it earns, and against it whatever (evil) it incurs.*' (2: 286) The first of these verses suggests that God holds people to account even for whatever thoughts may come into their minds, which they cannot stop. The second verse, which was revealed at a later date, suggests that He does not charge people with more than they can cope with. The fact is that the second verse explains and limits the meaning of the earlier one. It does not abrogate it. The truth is that God holds people to account only for what is within their ability, whether they make it known or keep it concealed. There is no case of abrogation here.[36]

Example 3: God says: '*The adulterer may marry none other than an adulteress or an idolatress; and the adulteress none may marry other than an adulterer or an idolater. That is forbidden to the believers.*' (24: 3) It is claimed that this verse is abrogated by what God says later in the same surah: '*Marry the single from among you as well as such of your male and female slaves as are virtuous. If they are poor, God will grant them sufficiency out of His bounty. God is Munificent, All-Knowing.*' (24: 32) The claim is made on the basis that the second verse came later. What this claim means is that

36. Al-Zurqānī, *Manāhil al-'Irfān*, vol. 2, p. 183.

the prohibition of marrying adulterous women is annulled by the fact that God makes it permissible to marry single Muslim women. That is certainly a strange understanding of the verses in question.[37] Al-Jassās, for example, comments on these verses: 'Scholars of all countries are agreed that it is permissible to marry [an adulteress] and that her adultery does not entail that it is forbidden to marry her... As such, the ruling stated in this verse [24: 3] is abrogated.'[38] Ibn al-Qayyim refutes this view, stating his scholarly view: 'As for marriage to an adulteress, God has made it clearly forbidden in surah 24, Light... It is clear that the claim that this ruling is abrogated is exceedingly weak.'[39] This is, methodologically, the correct view, because those who claim that the verse is abrogated have no basis for their claim except that the second verse was revealed later than the first, which does not necessarily support their case.

Example 4: It is claimed that the following ruling is abrogated: '*Those who find fasting a strain too hard to bear may compensate for it by feeding a needy person. He who does good of his own account does himself good thereby. For to fast is to do good to yourselves, if you only knew.*' (2: 184) The verse gives a person who finds fasting too hard a choice between fasting or paying compensation for it. It is claimed that this has been abrogated by the statement in the next verse: '*Therefore, whoever of you is present in that month shall fast throughout the month.*' (2: 185) This statement makes fasting obligatory and gives no choice. Al-Bukhārī relates that Ibn 'Umar read out God's words:

---

37. See, for example, the commentary on this verse in al-Qurṭubī, *Tafsīr*.
38. Al-Jassās, *Aḥkām al-Qur'ān*, vol. 5, p. 108. The prohibition of marriage to an adulteress is said here to be 'upheld only by Aḥmad'! Cf. Ibn Taymiyyah, *Kutub wa Rasā'il wa Fatāwā*, vol. 20, p. 229.
39. Ibn al-Qayyim, *Zād al-Ma'ād*, vol. 4, p. 7.

'may compensate for it [i.e. fasting] by feeding a needy person,' and said: 'This is abrogated'. Ibn 'Abbās said: 'It is not abrogated. It applies to an old man and an old woman who find fasting too hard: they may instead feed a needy person for every day they do not fast.'[40] Once again we see Ibn 'Abbās clarifying the operation of clear verses, each in its field, refuting the unsupported claims of abrogation.

Example 5: God says: '*It is prescribed for you, when death approaches any of you and he is leaving behind some property, to make bequests in favour of his parents and other near of kin in fairness. That is a duty incumbent on the God-fearing*.' (2: 180) This verse makes clear that giving bequests to one's parents and close relatives is obligatory for any Muslim who feels death approaching. However, it is claimed that this verse is abrogated, but scholars have different views about its abrogation, and which text abrogates it. The majority of scholars confirm that it is abrogated by the verses that give the details of the inheritance system (4: 11, 12 and 176), starting with: '*God has this to enjoin on you with regard to your children: The male shall have a share equal to that of two females*.'[41] (4: 11) It is also claimed that it is abrogated by the Hadith that says: 'No will may be made in favour of an heir.' Another version of this Hadith says: 'No will may be made in favour of an heir unless it is approved by all other heirs.' This Hadith does not meet al-Bukhārī's criteria of authenticity, but it is related by Abū Dāwūd and by al-Tirmidhī, who grades it as sound (*ḥasan*). It was a portion of the Prophet's address during his farewell pilgrimage, yet only Abū Umamah narrates it attributing it to the Prophet. This casts doubt on its authenticity, because

40. Al-Bukhārī, *Ṣaḥīḥ*, vol. 4, p. 1638.
41. Ibn Ḥajar, *Fatḥ al-Bārī*, vol. 5, p. 372; Ibn Rushd, *Bidāyat al-Mujtahid*, vol. 2, p. 251; Ibn Qudāmah, *al-Mughnī*, vol. 6, p. 57.

the Prophet's address was attended by thousands of his Companions and its being narrated by only one of them appears to me to raise a doubt. Al-Shāfi'ī cites this Hadith as evidence of abrogation,[42] even though his method states that the Qur'ān may not be abrogated by a Hadith. In any case, the majority of scholars agree that making a will in favour of an heir is permissible provided that all other heirs approve.[43] Tāwūs and other scholars say about this verse: 'It is not abrogated, but its application is made limited. "The near of kin" include a greater number of relatives than the heirs... The right of relatives who are not heirs remains intact.'[44] Therefore, the verse may be understood to refer to those relatives, including parents, who do not inherit (because of a particular reason such as difference in religion, according to some scholars). It may also be understood to refer to heirs with special circumstances that entitle them to greater care and kindness, such as being disabled, or weak, or having large families, and so on.[45] The fact that the verses detailing the system of inheritance were revealed later does not necessarily abrogate the ruling concerning the will unless there is clear evidence to suggest that. This is particularly true because the ruling concerning the will is confirmed by several other proofs. This gives us flexibility in dealing with the different circumstances of different heirs.

The Sunnah provides a large number of cases that are similar to our examples, in which scholars imagine two texts to be mutually contradictory and claim that the later one abrogates the earlier one. This they do despite the fact

42. Al-Shāfi'ī, *al-Umm*, vol. 4, p. 99.
43. Ibn Rushd, *Bidāyat al-Mujtahid*.
44. Muḥammad ibn 'Abd al-Bāqī al-Zurqānī, *Sharḥ al-Zurqānī 'alā al-Muwaṭṭa'*, vol. 4, p. 86.
45. Nadā, *al-Naskh fī al-Qur'ān*, p. 60.

that there is no clear statement indicating abrogation or annulment in any sense. Yet in every such case there are valid views expressed by some scholars, suggesting ways of reconciling such texts. There is no doubt that reconciliation is better, wherever possible.

It was obligatory for the Prophet's Companions to follow the most recent order, because they were with the Prophet (peace be upon him) and that was the proper course in the circumstances. He certainly knew best what was suitable for his community. Yet following the latest did not require them, and does not require us, to annul the earlier text, unless the Prophet clearly stipulated that. Some of them clearly understood this, as appears from the cited cases, which have been given only as examples. Thus we conclude that the Prophet's Companions were required to follow the latest orders given them by the Prophet; but this does not necessarily mean that the latest signifies the definitive annulment of previous orders, either in their case or in ours, unless a clear statement specifies that.

4. No abrogation based on anyone's personal opinion

In the light of what we have said so far, it may be added that we may not consider any view by a Companion of the Prophet or scholar, expressed on the basis of their own personal discretion and that might be corrected by others, as a 'text signifying abrogation', even though this may be found in books of Hadith. A view of a highly respected Companion of the Prophet or an eminent scholar is by no means 'a religious text' unless it quotes the words of the Legislator, or His messenger, expressing abrogation. Such a view is merely a personal opinion seeking to solve some superficial contradiction in a matter he might not have perfectly understood. Perfection belongs only to God and infallibility belongs to His Messenger (peace be upon him).

Scholars do not assign any validity to this sort of abrogation based on personal opinion, even though it may have been stated by a Companion of the Prophet. Commenting on the views of some, al-Shāfi'ī says in *Ikhtilāf al-Ḥadīth*: 'It is not right to accept the statement of whoever said that the Prophet did not wipe over his *khuffs* when performing the ablution at any time after the revelation of surah 5, The Repast. To accept his words, he must put them in a quotation from the Prophet. Otherwise, he is only stating what he knew. It is perfectly possible that other Companions might have known that the Prophet did wipe over his *khuffs* after the surah's revelation.'[46] He then added: 'There is no evidence to confirm abrogation except through an authentic report from God's Messenger.'[47] Al-Shawkānī said:

> Abrogation cannot be stated on the basis of probability. Besides, abrogation could only take place during the Prophet's lifetime, because abrogation must be stated in a religious text, and no such text can be made after the Prophet's death and the end of the revelation... How can something in the Qur'ān or in the Sunnah be discarded on the basis of personal opinion, or a statement by one of the Prophet's Companions or someone else? Scholars do not permit a ruling based on analogy to be discarded on the basis of a view expressed by a Companion of the Prophet. How could such a view be the basis of discarding something in the Book of God or the Prophet's Sunnah?[48]

In *al-Mustaṣfā*, Abū Ḥāmid al-Ghazālī said: 'No ruling may be abrogated on the strength of a Companion of the

46. Al-Shāfi'ī, *Ikhtilāf al-Ḥadīth*, vol. 1, p. 485.
47. Ibid., p. 487.
48. Al-Shawkānī, *Fatḥ al-Qadīr*, vol. 1, p. 305.

Prophet saying: "This ruling has been abrogated." One must say instead: "I heard God's Messenger (peace be upon him) say: 'I have abrogated this ruling'". If he says this, we consider the original ruling and if we find out that it is confirmed on the basis of single reporting, we rule that it is abrogated by the Companion's statement. If the original ruling is confirmed more absolutely then it is not abrogated. If a Companion says "This ruling is abrogated," his word is certainly unacceptable. He might have thought it so although the case cannot be one of abrogation. It happened that the mere addition to a statement was thought to constitute abrogation'.[49]

It is confirmed, then, that scholars have rejected claims of abrogation, even those made by Companions of the Prophet, unless they rely on an authentic statement by the Prophet. To reject similar claims by later scholars, who only rely on their views of superficial contradiction or their knowledge of the dates of events, is even more appropriate. The latter is merely an annulment of religious rulings on the basis of personal views.

Ibn Ḥajar makes the following comment on this approach to abrogation: 'To criticise confirmed reports on the strength of unfounded assumptions is unacceptable, and abrogation can only be accepted on solid evidence.'[50] Ibn Taymiyyah said: 'Abrogation can only be confirmed with certainty of evidence. No abrogation can be accepted on mere opinion.'[51] Ibn Rushd says: 'It is not permissible to disregard an item of legislation that we are required to implement merely on the basis of an assumption which we are not required to make the basis of abrogation… Assumptions that may serve as

49. Al-Ghazālī, *al-Mustaṣfā*, vol. 1, p. 103.
50. Ibn Ḥajar, *Fatḥ al-Bārī*, vol. 2, p. 363.
51. Ibn Taymiyyah, *Kutub wa Rasā'il wa Fatāwā*, vol. 21, p. 575.

foundations of rulings are well defined. These are rulings that need to be either withdrawn or acted upon. This does not apply to any assumption we make.'[52] Ibn Ḥazm said: 'It is not lawful for a Muslim to claim that any particular verse or Hadith is abrogated except on the basis of a text. It is a duty to obey God and obey His Messenger. If a statement of God or His Messenger is said to be abrogated, the duty to obey is removed, and this cannot be right. If anyone says that [the duty of] obedience to God and His Messenger is removed with regard to any part of Islamic law, their assertion is rejected unless he can prove it with an authentic text. If he produces such a text, we willingly accept it. If not, he is a liar telling falsehood.'[53]

Among the most peculiar claims of abrogation, without solid proof, are two cases that have had, and still have, serious legal effects. These are the claims of abrogation on the basis of two verses of the Qur'ān, known as the 'Verse of the Sword' and the 'Verse of the Screen'.

THE 'VERSE OF THE SWORD'

There are literally hundreds of claims of abrogation as a result of the 'Verse of the Sword', yet there are differences on defining which verse it is.[54] The most common view says that it is the verse that says: '*When these months of grace are over, slay the idolaters wherever you find them, and take them captive, besiege them, and lie in wait for them at every conceivable place. Yet if they should repent, take to prayer and pay the* Zakat, *let them go their way. For God is much-forgiving, ever merciful.*' (9: 5) It is claimed that this verse abrogated a large number of verses, including:

52. Ibn Rushd, *Bidāyat al-Mujtahid*, vol. 1, p. 63.
53. Ibn Ḥazm, *al-Iḥkām fī Uṣūl al-Aḥkām*, vol. 7, p. 380.
54. Qatādah al-Sadūsī et al., *Silsilat Kutub al-Nāsikh wa al-Mansūkh*.

- '*There shall be no compulsion in religion.*' (2: 256)
- '*So leave them to their own inventions.*' (6: 112)
- '*Repel evil with that which is better. We are fully aware of all that they say.*' (23: 96)
- '*As for those who have broken the unity of their faith and have become sects, you certainly have nothing to do with them. Their case rests with God.*' (6: 159)
- '*Should they argue with you, say: "God knows best what you are doing."*' (22: 68)
- '*So give respite to the unbelievers; leave them alone for a while.*' (86: 17)
- '*Speak kindly to people.*' (2: 83)
- '*Except those of them who have ties with people to whom you yourselves are bound by a covenant.*' (4: 90)
- '*If they incline to peace, incline to it as well, and place your trust in God.*' (8: 61)
- '*Is not God the most just of judges?*' (95: 8)

Since this last verse stresses one of God's attributes, it is a very strange example of the claims of abrogation without providing any evidence. Al-Qurṭubī, for example, says that 'it implies respect for a believer who acknowledges the existence of an ever-living Maker.' He then cites two views on this point. The first view suggests that the verse that says, 'Is not God the most just of judges?', is abrogated by the 'Verse of the Sword' because the latter 'abrogated all respect afforded to unbelievers,' according to al-Qurṭubī's understanding. The other view affirms that it is not abrogated, and is based on a report that when 'Alī heard this verse being recited, he said: 'Certainly, and I am witness to that.'[55] It is clear that both pieces of evidence, stating either abrogation or confirmation, lack any logical basis.

55. Al-Qurṭubī, *Tafsīr*, vol. 20, p. 117.

In any case, all these verses which we have mentioned are definitive and there is no contradiction between any of them and the so-called 'Verse of the Sword'. There is no evidence whatsoever to support the claims of abrogation, and as such none is abrogated. Unfortunately, these claims of abrogation by the 'Verse of the Sword' continue to be made by some members of some Islamic groups. As a result, they ignore all the texts that advocate good relations, wise advocacy of Islam, dialogue and freedom of belief. These ideas have led to the well-known disasters that have befallen Islam and the Muslim community.

The 'Verse of the Screen'

This is the verse that says: '*O you who believe, do not enter the Prophet's homes, unless you are given leave, for a meal without waiting for its proper time. But when you are invited, enter; and when you have eaten, disperse without lingering for the sake of mere talk. Such behaviour might give offence to the Prophet, and yet he might feel too shy to bid you go. God is not shy of stating what is right. When you ask the Prophet's wives for something, do so from behind a screen: that makes for greater purity for your hearts and theirs.*' (33: 53)

'Umar ibn al-Khaṭṭāb related, about the reason for its revelation: 'I said: "Messenger of God, people of all sorts come into your homes. Perhaps it will be appropriate that you order the Mothers of the Believers to stay behind a screen". God then revealed the Verse of the Screen.'[56] Another report suggested that the reason for its revelation was that a delegation visited the Prophet and ate at his house. One of them touched 'Ā'ishah's hand, and the Prophet did

56. Al-Bukhārī, *Ṣaḥīḥ*, vol. 5, p. 2303; vol. 4, pp. 1629, 1799.

not like this. Then the Verse of the Screen was revealed.[57] Although this verse clearly establishes the manners to be observed when entering the Prophet's homes, the claims of abrogation have made it a pretext for prohibiting, without evidence, everything God has permitted Muslim women in all times and places. Some scholars have claimed that it abrogated the permissibility of women leaving their homes. Ibn Taymiyyah claimed that this verse 'abrogated the permissibility of a woman showing her face to anyone other than her relatives whom she may not marry.'[58] Qāḍī 'Iyāḍ claimed that it abrogated [the permissibility of] women talking to men altogether.[59] Shams al-Ḥaqq al-'Aẓīm-Ābādī claimed that it abrogated the permissibility of a woman visiting and being visited by men.[60] Al-Mubārakfūrī even claimed that it abrogated the validity of women narrating Hadiths.[61] Concerning every one of these questions it has been said: 'This was before the revelation of the Verse of the Screen.' To accept such claims, which rely on no solid foundation or authentic evidence, would entail the abrogation of thousands of confirmed and authentic Hadiths that show the life of Muslim women and their status in the society established by the Prophet (peace be upon him).[62] This approach to the understanding of the 'Verse of the

57. Al-Qurṭubī, *Tafsīr*, vol. 14, p. 225.
58. Ibn Taymiyyah, *Kutub wa Rasā'il wa Fatāwā*, vol. 22, p. 110.
59. Al-Nawawī, *Sharḥ al-Nawawī 'alā Ṣaḥīḥ Muslim*, vol. 8, p. 184.
60. Al-'Aẓīm-Ābādī, *'Awn al-Ma'būd*, vol. 5, p. 263.
61. Al-Mubārakfūrī, *Tuḥfat al-Ahwadhī*, vol. 4, p. 179.
62. See, for example, 'Abd al-Ḥalīm Abū Shuqqah, *Taḥrīr al-Mar'ah fī 'Aṣr al-Risālah*, an extensive study which shows hundreds of portrayals of the exemplary norms of women's life in the Prophet's time. All these portrayals are drawn from the two authentic Hadith collections of al-Bukhārī and Muslim. Should we consider all these abrogated? May God bestow mercy on Abū Shuqqah. He had to put up with much abuse for stating the truth.

Screen' is a clear example of the erroneous method that declares the abrogation of clear religious texts because they are contrary to some biased and un-Islamic traditions that ill-treat women in some societies, or because they are contrary to a scholar's preconceived ideas.

A discussion of the only six abrogated verses identified in Dr Muṣṭafā Zayd's work

A number of eminent scholars have tried to limit the number of Qur'ānic verses which are claimed to have been abrogated. In his book *al-Itqān*, al-Suyūṭī limited the cases of abrogation to only twenty verses of the Qur'ān, some of which were abrogated by more than one verse, while others were abrogated by Hadiths.[63] A number of contemporary scholars are of the view that abrogation applies to a smaller number than the one suggested by al-Suyūṭī. These include Shaykh Muḥammad al-Khuḍarī, Dr Muṣṭafā Zayd, Shaykh 'Alī Ḥasab Allāh and Shaykh Muḥammad Abū Zuhrah.[64]

The most thorough research on this issue is that undertaken by the late Dr Muṣṭafā Zayd (may God bestow mercy on him). It is a highly scholarly and painstakingly study. He made a complete survey of the verses which are claimed to have been abrogated, then from the total he dropped the following:

- Seventy-five verses that are informative. Information cannot be abrogated.

63. According to al-Suyūṭī the following verses are abrogated: verses 115, 142, 180, 183, 187, 240 and 284 in surah 2; verses 8, 15 and 16 in surah 4; verse 65 in surah 8; verse 41 in surah 9; and verse 12 in surah 58.
64. See al-Khuḍarī, *Uṣūl al-Fiqh*; Zayd, *al-Naskh fī al-Qur'ān al-Karīm*; Ḥasab Allāh, *Uṣūl al-Tashrī' al-Islāmī*; Abū Zuhrah, *Uṣūl al-Fiqh*.

- Twenty-eight verses that give warnings. A warning cannot be abrogated.
- Forty-eight verses that demarcate, limit or explain statements. To these the term 'abrogation' cannot apply.
- Sixty-three verses are claimed to have been abrogated although no contradiction has been established between what is abrogating and what is abrogated. He studied these in detail.
- Sixty-three other definitive verses are claimed to have been abrogated by the 'Verse of the Sword', but no evidence of such abrogation has been provided.

He concluded that there are six verses which he said: 'Are agreed upon by all who have written about abrogation.'[65] Although these scholarly works, particularly that of Muṣṭafā Zayd, have limited to a great extent the claims of abrogation that lack evidence and proof, they continue to adopt the method of claiming abrogation in order to solve a superficial contradiction between verses, without providing clear evidence. With great respect to Shaykh Muṣṭafā Zayd, I propose to undertake an analysis of these six verses in a way that corrects this methodology and implements the legal theoretical conclusion I have explained in this book.

A VERSE THAT LINKS THE HARDER TASK TO SITUATIONS OF STRENGTH AND THE LESSER ONE TO SITUATIONS OF WEAKNESS.

The verse concerned is: '*Prophet, urge the believers to fight. If there are twenty steadfast men among you, they will overcome two hundred, and if there are a hundred of you, they will defeat a thousand of those who disbelieve; for those are devoid of understanding*.' (8: 65) There is no abrogation of this verse, but Dr Muṣṭafā Zayd said that it

65. Zayd, ibid., vol. 2, p. 847.

was abrogated by the next verse: '*Now God has lightened your burden, for He knows that you are weak. So if there are a hundred steadfast men among you, they shall overcome two hundred; and if there are a thousand of you they shall, by God's will, defeat two thousand. God is with those who are steadfast.*' (8: 66)

Dr Yūsuf al-Qaradāwī refers to these two verses under the subheading: 'Qur'ānic evidence that rulings may change according to time, place and circumstances'. He says:

> Careful reading of God's book shows that this rule has a basis in the Qur'ān. This occurs in a number of verses that many commentators claim to be either abrogating others or abrogated by them. For certain, they are neither, but each has its own field of operation. The one may represent strength while the other addresses weakness... The meaning of these two verses, as explained by the author of *al-Manār*, is that the lowest condition of believers is that in which one hundred of them will overpower two hundred of their enemy and one thousand will win against two thousand. This is specifically related to their condition of weakness... God commands them to always be in a situation of strength so that they may fight an enemy which outnumbers them by ten times or more. Were the Muslims able to defeat the Byzantines and the Persians except on this basis?... Some commentators argue that the verse mentioning the case of strength was abrogated by the one that follows giving a concession, as it clearly states that God has lightened their burden. However, a concession does not contradict the case of strength, particularly as it is clearly stated in this verse that there was a case of weakness. Abrogation does not come at the same time as the original order and before it can be acted upon. It also appears that the two verses were revealed at the same time.[66]

---

66. Al-Qaradāwī, *Madkhal li-Dirāsat al-Sharī'at al-Islāmiyyah*, pp. 202–3.

Thus, Shaykh al-Qaradāwī links the easier ruling stated in the second verse to its cause, which is the state of weakness. Therefore, it applies in cases of weakness but not in cases of strength. He did not approve the complete annulment of the first ruling. In this way, he implements both verses and rejects the claims of abrogation. This ruling comes under the objectives of leadership which I discuss in this book.

A verse intended to identify hypocrites within the community of the Prophet's Companions

Dr Muṣṭafā Zayd stated that the following verse was abrogated: '*Believers, when you wish to speak to God's Messenger in private, offer something in charity before you speak to him. That is better for you and more conducive to purity. If you do not have the means, God is much-forgiving, ever merciful.*' (58: 12) He considered that the ruling specified in this verse was abrogated by the very next verse: '*Do you hesitate to offer charity before you speak with the Prophet? Since you did not offer charity, and God has turned to you in His mercy, attend regularly to prayer and pay your* Zakat *[i.e. obligatory charity] and obey God and His Messenger. God is well aware of your actions.*' (58: 13)

There is no unanimity among scholars that the first of these two verses was abrogated. Indeed, many of them reject the claim of abrogation, but they give three different explanations. Some say that the first verse does not specify a duty, but recommends giving some charity before speaking to the Prophet (peace be upon him). If it is a recommendation, it is not annulled. Others hold that the ruling given in the first verse cannot be described as 'abrogated' or 'annulled' because it was never implemented by anyone. A third group suggests that the first ruling had a definite aim other than a charitable donation, and it was achieved. This appears to me to be the correct view.

Shaykh Muḥammad al-Khuḍarī, for example, said about the claim of abrogation: 'The first of these two verses made it imperative to offer charity when one wished to speak to the Prophet, but the second verse removed this imperative without stating that it had been removed.'[67] The same view is expressed by Ibn Kathīr, who states that the order was to show the desirability of paying charity, without making it compulsory.[68] It seems to me, however, that the wording of the second verse suggests a duty, not a recommendation: 'Do you hesitate to offer charity...?' Al-Qurṭubī takes a different view, saying that no abrogation was due, because the first verse was never implemented. He rejects the report that 'Alī was the only one of the Prophet's Companions who acted on the first verse. Al-Qurṭubī says: 'What is reported about 'Alī is not authentic, because God says in the second verse "Since you did not offer charity," and this suggests that no one gave any charity.' However, the narration about 'Alī acting on this verse is authentic, related by al-Ḥākim in *al-Mustadrak*: 'Alī ibn Abī Ṭālib said: "There is a verse in God's book which no one else ever implemented and none will ever implement after me. It is the verse concerning speaking to the Prophet: 'Do you hesitate to offer charity before you speak with the Prophet?'..."' Al-Ḥākim said: 'This Hadith is authentic, meeting the criteria of al-Bukhārī and Muslim, but neither related it.' The third view links the verses to a particular reason, which is the need to distinguish hypocrites in society in Madīnah. [Abū Bakr] Ibn al-'Arabī said:

67. Al-Ghazālī, *Naẓarāt fī al-Qur'ān*, p. 211.
68. Ibn Kathīr, *Tafsīr*, vol. 2, p. 4.

> The hypocrites used to say that Muḥammad was like an ear listening to anyone who speaks to him. God revealed the verse that says: '*And among them are others who hurt the Prophet and say: "He is all ear." Say: "He is an ear listening to what is good for you."*' (9: 61) In reference to this, God also says: '*Believers, when you converse in secret, do not do so with a view to sinful doings, aggressive conduct and disobedience of God's Messenger, but rather hold counsel to promote righteousness and God-consciousness. Always remain God-fearing; to Him you will be gathered. [All other kinds of] secret conversation is the work of Satan, designed to cause grief to the believers. Yet he cannot harm them in the least, unless it be by God's leave. In God, then, let the believers place their trust.*' (58: 9–10) They did not stop to speak to the Prophet. Hence God revealed: '*Believers, when you wish to speak to God's Messenger in private, offer something in charity before you speak to him. That is better for you and more conducive to purity.*' (58: 12) God wanted the people of falsehood to stop coming to the Prophet and speaking to him. God knew that such false people would not offer charity to speak to the Prophet. This put an end to their coming to the Prophet. However, the order was felt to be too hard by believers who needed to speak to the Prophet. They complained to him and said that they could not manage it. God then stated that it was removed.[69]

Abū Muslim expressed the same view: 'This was removed because its cause was removed. Implementing this verse as an aspect of worship aimed to distinguish the hypocrites from the believers.'[70] This is an explanation of the ruling by its purpose, which was to distinguish Muslims from unbelievers. As the reason for the ruling no longer applies,

69. Ibn al-'Arabī, *Aḥkām al-Qur'ān*, vol. 4, p. 202.
70. See the commentary on this verse in al-Rāzī, *Mafātīḥ al-Ghayb*.

the ruling itself does not apply. It is not a question of abrogating an earlier ruling by a later one.

FOUR OTHER CASES SIGNIFYING GRADUAL LEGISLATION

Case 1: God says: '*O Believers, intoxicants, games of chance, idolatrous practices and divining arrows are abominations devised by Satan, so turn away from them so that you may be successful.*' (5: 90) This is the verse that gives the final ruling prohibiting all intoxicants.

Case 2: God says: '*You enfolded one, stand in prayer at night, all but a small part of it, half of it, or a little less, or add to it. Recite the Qur'ān calmly and distinctly.*' (73: 1–4) It is claimed that the ruling in these verses is abrogated by the last verse in the surah which says: '*Your Lord knows that you stand in prayer nearly two-thirds of the night, or one-half or one-third of it, as do some of your followers. It is God who determines the measure of night and day. He is aware that you will not be able to keep a measure of it, and therefore He turns towards you in His grace. Recite of the Qur'ān as much as may be easy for you. He knows that some of you will be sick, others will go about in the land seeking God's bounty, and others will be fighting for God's cause. Therefore, recite whatever you may do with ease.*' (73: 20)

Case 3: God says: '*Believers, fasting is decreed for you as it was decreed for those before you, so that you may be God-fearing.*' (2: 183) It is said that this verse implies that we are required to implement the legislation that was in force for believers before Islam, which meant that sexual intercourse between man and wife was prohibited after sleeping on a night of fasting. It is further claimed that it was abrogated by the verse that begins '*It is lawful for you to be intimate with your wives during the night preceding the fast.*' (2: 187)

Case 4: It is claimed that the following two verses were abrogated: '*As for those of your women who are guilty of gross immoral conduct, call upon four from among you to bear witness against them. If they so testify, then confine the guilty women to their houses until death takes them or God opens another way for them. And the two from among you who are guilty of the same, punish them both. If they repent and mend their ways, then leave them alone. God is the accepter of repentance, Ever-Merciful.*' (4: 15–16) Dr Zayd said that they were abrogated by the following verse: '*As for the adulteress and the adulterer, flog each of them with a hundred stripes.*' (24: 2) This appears to be yet another example of a step-by-step method to ultimately arrive at the final ruling. Thus it is by no means a case of complete annulment that prevents its implementation under any circumstances.

Which punishment for adultery?

We need to put in context the verse speaking about flogging as punishment for adultery: '*As for the adulteress and the adulterer, flog each of them with a hundred stripes.*' (24: 2) It should be taken together with, not in isolation of, other rulings applicable to this offence. For example, if a judge determines that the mandatory punishment may be waived as a result of the offender's repentance, he may pardon that offender or enforce the verses that prescribe a lesser punishment. The following verses announce God's ruling about how to deal with those who wage war against God and His Messenger: '*It is but a just punishment for those who make war on God and His Messenger and endeavour to spread corruption on earth, that they be put to death, or be crucified, or have their hands and feet cut off on alternate sides or that they be banished from the land. Such is their disgrace in this world, and more grievous suffering awaits them in the life to come; except those who repent before you overpower them. For you must know that God is much-forgiving, ever-merciful.*' (5: 33–4) Scholars are unanimous that the mandatory punishment for this offence of waging war against God and His Messenger is dropped if the offender repents. How about repentance by offenders who commit lesser crimes for which God has specified lesser punishments?[71]

The proper answer, and the view that meets the objectives of mandatory punishments, is that repentance, when expressed and confirmed by other circumstances, should be accepted. This should at least be a general rule. Dr Tawfīq al-Shāwī expresses a similar point of view:

> It is clear that the Prophet's Sunnah gives every encouragement to offenders to repent. It goes as far as advising the one who confesses his guilt to retract his confession and thus confirm his repentance. This broad perspective of repentance is overlooked by many people... Yet it is a more effective way of combating crime, reforming offenders and improving society than the enforcement of stipulated punishments. When the accused declares his repentance, and his seriousness is confirmed, this should be considered by the judge as a reason to refrain from imposing the maximum punishment, whether it be mandatory or retaliatory... However, repentance does not exempt the offender from civil liabilities... A probationary

71. For an expostulation of the views of different schools of *fiqh*, see 'Abd al-Qādir Awdah, *al-Tashrī' al-Jinā'ī al-Islāmī*, chapter on what prevents the enforcement of mandatory punishments.

> period may be established as a means to encourage the accused to repent. As such, it is perfectly consistent with our Islamic law and its objectives.[72]

Professor Muḥammad Salim al-Awa, who specialises in this field, also endorses the acceptance of repentance to waive mandatory punishments. He writes:

> The argument in support of dropping mandatory punishments as a result of repentance, or giving the repentant offender a pardon, is stronger than the argument against it… The objection that this opens the door for every offender to pretend that he or she has repented is not to be entertained. When we say that repentance is a reason for waiving punishment, we are not saying that the judge should not look carefully at such repentance to practically determine whether it is genuine or not.[73]

A related question pertaining to these verses and the question of abrogation is that of stoning. Most scholars are of the view that stoning is the established punishment for a married adulterer. However, a different view suggests that stoning was part of the Jewish law which Islam abrogated by the above-mentioned verse specifying flogging as punishment. As such, stoning is not part of Islamic law. The relevant verses are not abrogated, but they abrogate parts of the Jewish law. A different view suggests that the verse specifying flogging is definitive and general, while stoning is a discretionary punishment that the judge may enforce.

---

72. Al-Shāwī's opinion is quoted in Awdah, *al-Mawsū'at al-'Aṣriyyah fī al-Fiqh al-Jinā'ī al-Islāmī*, chapter on initiation, participation and repentance.
73. For further details, see Muḥammad Salim al-Awa, *Fī Uṣūl al-Niẓām al-Jina'ī al-Islāmī*.

Both views should be carefully considered in our present circumstances. They are mentioned by Shaykh Yūsuf al-Qaradāwī and other contemporary scholars. Al-Qaradāwī wrote:

> At this conference held in Libya in 1972, Shaykh [Muḥammad] Abū Zuhrah said what was a bombshell when he surprised the participants with his previously unexpressed view. Addressing the conference, he said: 'I have kept to myself a certain point of view I have had on a question of *fiqh* for more than twenty years. I have only expressed it to Dr 'Abd al-'Azīz Amīr.' At this point he sought Dr Amīr's confirmation and asked him: 'Is it not so, Dr 'Abd al-Azīz?' Dr Amīr confirmed that it was. Shaykh Abū Zuhrah went on: 'It is time that I stated openly what I have been keeping to myself, because I fear that when I meet my Lord He will ask me: "Why did you conceal your knowledge and did not explain it to people?" This view of mine is concerned with the question of the stoning punishment in the case of a married adulterer. My view is that stoning was part of the Jewish law, which was applied by God's Messenger before it was abrogated by the verse in surah 24 replacing it by the flogging punishment. I base my view on three different pieces of evidence. The first is that God says [concerning slave girls guilty of adultery]: "*If after their marriage, they are guilty of gross immoral conduct, they shall be liable to half the punishment to which free women are liable.*" (4: 25) As a penalty, stoning cannot be halved. Therefore, this verse refers to the punishment mentioned in surah 24, Light: "*As for the adulteress and the adulterer, flog each of them with a hundred stripes, and let not compassion for them keep you from [carrying out] this law of God, if you truly believe in God and the Last Day; and let a number of believers witness their punishment.*" (24: 2) The second piece of evidence is

the Hadith related by al-Bukhārī in his authentic Hadith anthology on the authority of 'Abd Allāh ibn Awfā, who said that he was asked about the stoning punishment: "Was it before or after the revelation of surah 24?" He said that he did not know. Therefore, it is highly likely that the stoning punishment was done before it was abrogated by the verse in surah 24. My third piece of evidence is that Hadith scholars rely upon a Hadith which states that the stoning punishment was specified in a verse of the Qur'ān the text of which was abrogated but the ruling of which remained in force. This is something that defies logic. Why should the text be removed when the ruling it specifies remains in force? It is further said that this was in [the Companion's] document but a hen ate it. This defies all logic.' When Shaykh Abū Zuhrah finished his discourse, most participants expressed their vehement disagreement. Those who spoke simply quoted what is stated in books of *fiqh* concerning these three pieces of evidence. Shaykh Abū Zuhrah, however, remained unmoved.

When the session was over, I spoke to him privately. I said: 'Your honour, I have a view which is close to yours but which will perhaps raise less objection.' He asked me to explain. I said: 'An authentic Hadith [on the punishment for adultery] says: "For a virgin man and a virgin woman: one hundred stripes and exile for a year; and for a married man and a married woman: one hundred stripes and stoning."' He asked me what I understood from this Hadith. I said: 'You know that the Ḥanafī school of *fiqh* says about the first part of the Hadith that the flogging is the mandatory punishment, but the exile is a matter of discretion that is up to the ruler to enforce. It does not apply in all cases…' However, Shaykh Abū Zuhrah did not agree with me. He said: 'Yūsuf, do you think that Muḥammad ibn 'Abd Allāh, whom God made His Messenger of mercy to all worlds, could have ordered the stoning of people to death? This is a Jewish

> law…' I thought: how many scholarly and daring views remain unexpressed by their holders and then die with them, because no one reports such views![74]

Shaykh 'Iṣām Talīmah wrote a comprehensive essay on this question, in which he says:

> Some experts say that stoning is a discretionary punishment that is up to the ruler to enforce, as he considers the best course of action to serve the interests of the Muslim community. Some of these authorities expressed their point of view in detail, citing the evidence they relied upon. Such scholars include 'Abd al-Wahhāb Khallāf, Muḥammad Abū Zuḥrah, Muḥammad al-Bannā, Muṣṭafā al-Zarqā, Yūsuf al-Qaradāwī and Muḥammad Su'ād Jalāl. Others expressed the same view, but it was reported from these scholars without the evidence they cited. This occurred because the scholar might have mentioned it verbally, or he might have mentioned it to some of his students, or expressed it in a session but the discussion was not documented. These experts include Maḥmūd Shalṭūṭ, 'Alī al-Khafīf and 'Alī Ḥasab Allāh.[75]

Be that as it may, we conclude that abrogation cannot be assumed on the basis of imagined contradiction between definitive verses of the Qur'ān. Indeed, such definitive verses should be understood within the overall framework of the theme to which they relate. Only in this way can a scholar explain how they are to be applied in practice. Moreover, abrogation which means total annulment that applies to religious rulings specified in religious texts cannot

74. Yūsuf al-Qaradāwī's diaries, 'Ibn al-Qaryah wa al-Kuttāb': http://www.qaradāwī.net
75. From an electronic copy the author kindly provided me with. See, http://www.leadersta.com

be claimed without clear evidence. Verses of the Qur'ān may abrogate rulings that operated in earlier Divine laws, but these verses may not be abrogated. Abrogation in this sense of final annulment may be confirmed by 'express wording', as scholars say. This is what we are to discuss now.

5. What does 'express' abrogation mean? Is it enough to prohibit something after it was permissible, or to permit it after it was prohibited?

Scholars of legal theory, or *uṣūl al-fiqh*, have discussed the limits of abrogation on the basis of the variance in the degrees of authenticity of abrogating and abrogated texts. Scholars differ as to whether a verse of the Qur'ān may be abrogated by a Hadith, and the degree of authenticity required for such an abrogating Hadith, if abrogation by a Hadith is acceptable. Al-Shāfi'ī maintains that nothing of the Qur'ān may be abrogated except by another Qur'ānic text. His evidence is clearly the verse that says: '*Any revelation We annul or consign to oblivion We replace with a better or similar one*.' (2: 106) Al-Shāfi'ī also says that the Sunnah can only be abrogated by the Sunnah, and his evidence is arrived at through a process of induction.[76]

Ibn Surayj and Abū al-Khaṭṭāb are of the view that rulings in the Qur'ān may be abrogated by a Hadith of the grade of 'multiple transmission' (*mutawātir*) because it is of the same degree of authenticity. However, they believe that although possible [in principle] it did not take place. Most theologians and Abū Ḥanīfah maintain such abrogation of a Qur'ānic ruling by a recurrent Hadith is acceptable and that there were examples of this. The same is reported of Mālik

76. Al-Shāfi'ī, *al-Risālah*, pp. 108–9.

and theologians belonging to the Mu'tazilah and Ash'arī schools. Some scholars of the Ẓāhirī school consider that a Hadith, even if singly reported, may abrogate a Qur'ānic ruling.[77]

Whichever view is correct, abrogation, in the sense of final annulment, is the prerogative of God, the Legislator, alone. Such annulment must be understood from the clear meaning of the abrogating text, whether it is a Qur'ānic verse or a Hadith, and whether it is of the recurrent grade or not. The question is: what is an 'express wording' that removes a religious ruling and entails its abrogation? Abū Ḥāmid al-Ghazālī defines what he calls 'express abrogation' as 'a statement by a Companion of the Prophet saying: "I heard God's Messenger (peace be upon him) say: 'I hereby abrogate such-and-such ruling.'"'[78]

However, a survey of the Prophet's Hadiths confirms that no derivation of the Arabic root *nasakha*, which means 'abrogate', ever occurred in his statements. I undertook a separate research study on this point and I confirm that no such word has ever occurred in any Hadith graded as authentic or good and entered into the compilations of al-Bukhārī, Muslim, al-Tirmidhī, al-Nasā'ī, Abū Dāwūd, Ibn Mājah, or in Aḥmad's *Musnad*, Mālik's *Muwaṭṭa'*, al-Ḥākim's *Mustadrak*, or the collections of al-Dārimī, Ibn Ḥibbān, Ibn al-Jarūd, Ibn Khuzaymah, al-Bayhaqī, al-Dāraquṭnī, or al-Shāfi'ī's *Musnad*. I found it in the statements of narrators or commentators, or titles of chapters in these books under forty different topics.

The only exception is a narration included by al-Bayhaqī, al-Dāraquṭnī and others on the authority of Masrūq, reporting from 'Alī, which says: 'Zakat abrogates every

77. Ibn Taymiyyah, *al-Muswaddah fī Uṣūl al-Fiqh*, vol. 1, p. 182.
78. Al-Ghazālī, *al-Mustaṣfā*, vol. 1, p. 182.

charity; the grand ablution abrogates every ablution; fasting in Ramadan abrogates every fast; and the sacrifice on the [ʻĪd] al-Aḍḥā abrogates every sacrifice.'[79] However, the text of this narration is clearly flimsy, needing no comment. As for its chain of transmission, we quote the comments by al-Maqdisī[80] and others: 'It is narrated by Mūsāyyab ibn Shārik, from ʻUtbah ibn Yaẓāan, from al-Shaʻbī, from Masrūq, from ʻAlī. Thus it is narrated by Musayyab, and scholars are unanimous that he was a liar and his narrations are to be discarded.'

Al-Ghazālī then gives two examples of what he calls 'clear expression of abrogation'. These are, 'I had prohibited the preservation of sacrificial meat; but now you may preserve it', and 'I had prohibited visiting graves of the dead; but now you may visit them'. This means that al-Ghazālī considered an expression of prohibition of something that was earlier permitted, or an expression of permission of something that was earlier prohibited, equal to a clear: 'I hereby abrogate such-and-such ruling',[81] in that both are clear expressions of abrogation by the Prophet (peace be upon him). This is the view of the majority of scholars. It is also the majority view that such 'clear expression' is confirmed by what is thought to be abrogating and what is thought to be abrogated within the same context, as in the two mentioned examples.[82]

---

79. ʻAlī ibn Aḥmad al-Dāraquṭnī, *Sunan al-Dāraquṭnī*, vol. 4, p. 281.
80. Muḥammad ibn Ṭāhir al-Maqdisī, *Dhakhīrat al-Ḥuffāẓ*, vol. 5, p. 2480.
81. Al-Ghazālī, *Al-Mustaṣfā*, vol. 1, p. 101.
82. See, for example, al-Ḥāzimī, *al-Iʻtibār fī al-Nāsikh wa al-Mansūkh fī al-Ḥadīth*, vol. 1, p. 59; Ibn Ḥajar, *Fatḥ al-Bārī*, vol. 10, p. 25; Ibn ʻAbd al-Barr, *al-Istidhkār*, vol. 5, p. 233; al-Zurqānī, *Sharḥ al-Zurqānī ʻalā al-Muwaṭṭa'*, vol. 3, p. 100; al-Sarakhsī, *Uṣūl al-Sarakhsī*, vol. 2, p. 77; al-Āmidī, *al-Aḥkām*, vol. 3, p. 148; Ibn Amīr al-Ḥajj, *al-Taqrīr wa al-Taḥbīr*, vol. 3, p. 77; al-Jassās, *al-Fuṣūl fī*

To analyse this theory, we will discuss the two reports in which al-Ghazālī's two examples occur.

Narration 1: Mālik relates in *al-Muwaṭṭa'* on the authority of Abū Sa'īd al-Khudrī that he returned from a journey, and his family served him some meat to eat. He said: 'Check whether this is sacrificial meat.' They told him that it was so. Abū Sa'īd said: 'Has not God's Messenger prohibited this?' They said: 'But God's Messenger subsequently said something else.' Abū Sa'īd went out and enquired. He was told that God's Messenger (peace be upon him) had said: 'I prohibited you to eat sacrificial meat after three days, but now you may eat it, give it in charity and preserve it. I also prohibited making drinks, but now you may make them; but beware, for every intoxicant is forbidden. I also prohibited visiting graves, but now you may visit them – but do not say vulgar words.'[83]

Narration 2: A different narration of the same event is stated by Anas. It says: 'The Prophet prohibited visiting graves, eating sacrificial meat after three days, and brewing drinks in [containers known as] *al-Dubba'*, *al-Ḥantam* and *al-Muzaffat*. Three days later, God's Messenger (peace be upon him) said: "I forbade you three things, but then I have been thinking about them. I prohibited you visiting graves, but now I think that such visits soften hearts, make eyes tearful and remind people of the Day of Judgement. Therefore, visit them but do not say vulgar words. I also prohibited eating the meat of sacrifice after three nights, but

---

al-Uṣūl, vol. 2, p. 281; Ibn Qudamah, *Rawḍat al-Nāẓir*, vol. 1, p. 182; al-Sam'ānī, *Qawāṭi' al-Adillah fī al-Uṣūl*, vol. 1, p. 429; Ibn Kathīr, *Tuḥfat al-Ṭālib*, vol. 1, p. 373; al-'Aẓīm-Ābādī, *'Awn al-Ma'būd*, vol. 8, p. 7.

83. Mālik, *al-Muwaṭṭa'*, vol. 2, p. 485. It is an authentic Hadith related in slightly different versions by Muslim, Abū Dāwūd, al-Tirmidhī, al-Nasā'ī and Ibn Mājah.

now I think that people may retain [some] for themselves, serve their guests and keep [some] for absent relatives. Therefore, keep what you wish. I also prohibited you brewing your drinks in those containers, but you may drink from whatever containers you wish, but do not drink any intoxicant. Anyone may cover his drinking-bottle on what is sinful.'"[84]

The questions that need to be answered here are these. Is such clear expression of prohibiting something after it had been permitted, or permitting it after it had been prohibited, sufficient to rule that the original ruling has been abrogated and finally annulled, so as not to be implemented in any situation? If we know the reason for the ruling, either from the text or through scholarly effort, does such knowledge affect our verdict of abrogation? For example, the Prophet (peace be upon him) said that his prohibition of eating the meat of sacrifice after three days was 'for the sake of those people who had arrived'.[85] On the other hand, scholars deduced that visiting graves was forbidden because the Arabs used to make it a pretext for boasting about their own numbers. When Islam was well established in their hearts, the prohibition was relaxed.[86] In such cases, should we link a ruling to its reason, so that the ruling applies when the reason exists, but does not apply in its absence? Or is the change permanent, which is the accepted meaning of abrogation? How important is the objective of each of the two rulings, if such objectives are identified either through a clear statement or careful consideration? The answers to all these questions are determined by looking at the objectives and meanings of texts.

---

84. Abū Ya'lā Aḥmad ibn 'Alī al-Tamīmī, *al-Musnad*, vol. 6, p. 373.
85. Muslim, *Ṣaḥīḥ*, vol. 3, p. 1561.
86. Al-Zurqānī, *Sharḥ al-Zurqānī 'alā al-Muwaṭṭa'*, vol. 3, p. 101.

Chapter Five

Cases of how Objectives Help in the Enforcement of Superficially Contradictory Texts

1. Objectives of protecting the approved essentials by the Muslim government

THE HADITHS quoted included rulings of permission that have been considered to abrogate earlier rulings of prohibition regarding three matters: using sacrificial meat after three days, brewing drinks in any type of container unless the drink causes intoxication, and visiting graves. However, other narrations cite causes for the Prophet's earlier prohibition of these matters.

Muslim gives the following title to a chapter in his *Ṣaḥīḥ* collection: 'The prohibition of eating sacrificial meat after three days in the early days of Islam and explaining its abrogation for good.' He then mentions the Hadith in which the Prophet says: 'I only prohibited it because of the travellers who arrived [at the time]. [Now] you may eat of it, keep and give in charity.' The wording of the Hadith specifies the reason for the prohibition: it being the group of poor people who arrived in Madīnah.[1] In her narration of the same event, 'Ā'ishah said: 'Some Bedouins arrived in Madīnah.'[2] In a different narration 'Ābis ibn Rabī'ah said: 'I asked 'Ā'ishah: "Did the Prophet prohibit eating the meat of sacrifice after three days?" She said: "He only did it in a year when people were hungry, and he wanted the rich to feed the poor... Only a small number of people used to sacrifice. He prohibited it so that whoever offered a sacrifice would give meat to those who did not."'[3] If we look at this question from the point of view of the reason, we realise that the reason for the prohibition, which is the passage of three days, is consistent with the ruling of prohibition and contrary to the ruling of permission. Hence the majority of scholars deemed that this perceived contradiction amounts to abrogation. However, 'Ā'ishah did not find any contradiction or abrogation in the whole matter. She explained that the prohibition was not meant as forbidding such meat. Its objective was merely to ease a difficult situation. Hence she said: 'He did not actually make [the meat] forbidden to eat, but he wanted to provide for the travellers who arrived in Madīnah.'[4]

This, then, is a clear text stating that the reason for the earlier prohibition was not the mere passage of three days, but the need to provide for some needy Muslims. That is indeed the underlying reason for the Divine order on this point, as God says: '*so that they might experience much that shall be of benefit to them, and that they might extol the name of God on the days appointed [for sacrifice], over whatever heads of cattle He may have provided for them. Eat, then,*

1. Al-Zurqānī, *Sharḥ al-Zurqānī 'alā al-Muwaṭṭa'*, vol. 3, p. 99.
2. Ibid.
3. Ibn Ḥajar, *Fatḥ al-Bārī*, vol. 10, p. 25.
4. Aḥmad ibn Muḥammad al-Ṭahāwī, *Sharḥ Ma'ānī al-Āthār*, vol. 4, p. 188.

of such [sacrificed cattle] and feed the unfortunate poor.' (22: 28) The Prophet ordered the people not to keep any meat from their sacrifice after three days, not as a means intending this as a total prohibition, but as a means to ensure the feeding of the needy and to provide for them, as 'Ā'ishah explained. Therefore, if the same cause arises again and we definitely know the objective of the ruling, we must apply the ruling. The point is that the ruling is intertwined with the cause: when the latter exists, the ruling applies, and vice versa. Expressing the same opinion, al-Shāfi'ī said: 'If a large number of people arrive, the prohibition of keeping the meat of sacrifice for more than three days applies. If not, then the concession to eat, keep, and give in charity also applies.'[5] Shaykh Aḥmad Shākir comments on al-Shāfi'ī's words: 'This is a fine way of looking at matters, requiring reflection, insight and thorough knowledge of the Qur'ān and the Sunnah and their meaning. To apply this is often very difficult, except for those to whom God grants guidance.'[6]

Therefore, if some poor refugees arrive in a country, as happened in Madīnah that year, it is the duty of those who offer sacrifice at the time of the Eid to feed them from their sacrifice and not to retain any portion of such meat after three days. This is especially applicable if such poor people are hungry, as was the case in Madīnah and as is the case in many places these days.

If we try to broaden the area of deduction so as to go beyond abrogation and explanation and look further at the general objective of the narrations regarding meat from sacrifices, we find in these Hadiths further indications and suitable evidence. We may conclude that a Muslim ruler has

5. Al-Shāfi'ī, *al-Risālah*, vol. 1, p. 239.
6. Ibid., p. 242 (footnote).

the authority, and indeed the duty, to put in place measures to help secure the essentials defined by Islam. Such measures may aim at protecting people from hunger, by encouraging the concept of mutual care in the Muslim community, and balancing that against the principle of freedom of ownership and the private use of what one owns, when the community has no urgent need for such resources of individual members. This way of understanding Islamic rulings brings us closer to the religious and political understanding shown by the rightly guided Caliphs, particularly 'Umar ibn al-Khaṭṭāb. It will help us in understanding religious texts so as to build an Islamic society that balances the rights of the individual against national interests in the light of the objectives of Islamic law.

Let us now look at the second part of the Hadith which is concerned with brewing drinks. Muslim's narration on the authority of 'Ā'ishah adds some details: 'The delegation from the 'Abd al-Qays tribe visited the Prophet and asked him about brewing drinks. He prohibited them to brew in *al-Dubba'*, *al-Naqīr*, *al-Muzaffat* and *al-Ḥantam*.' This was the first prohibition. However, Ibn Ḥibbān's entry in his *Ṣaḥīḥ* sheds more light on the occasion when this prohibition was made, linking it to the delegation's conversation with the Prophet. Under the chapter headed 'The reason why drinking out of *al-Ḥantam* is prohibited', Ibn Ḥibbān enters on Abū Hurayrah's authority: 'God's Messenger prohibited the 'Abd al-Qays delegation to brew in *al-Dubba'*, *al-Ḥantam*, *al-Muzaffat*, *al-Naqīr* or a leather bottle cut from the top. He said: "Brew your drink in your usual bottle and cover it, so that you have your drink sweet and pleasant." One man said: "Messenger of God, permit me this little" – al-Nadr [the narrator] pointed with his hand. The Prophet said: "Then you will make it this much" – al-Nadr pointed with his arm.' Abū Ḥātim said: 'The man's request was that the Prophet should allow brewing a small amount in such containers, but the Prophet did not permit that for fear that he would use that in excess, which would lead to drinking an intoxicating quantity.'[7]

If we consider the reason for the prohibition to be the containers themselves, we end up with a perceived contradiction that leads to a ruling of abrogation. But if we look at the objective, we realise that those people used these particular types of container to brew their alcoholic drinks. The Prophet wanted to train his Companions by stopping the means of making intoxicants for a period of time. When they abandoned such drinks, he established the overall rule which states that every intoxicant drink is forbidden. This understanding is supported by Ibn Mājah's narration of the Hadith permitting the use of such containers. It adds: 'Containers do not make anything unlawful, but any intoxicant drink is unlawful.'[8] Needless to say, what intoxicates is a drink that influences the mind.

The whole matter, then, is one of training and education, with the aim of protecting one's mental ability through removing what invites people to drink intoxicants in the first place. Hence, the second ruling did not annul the first. Indeed, the first ruling remains valid whenever conditions or circumstances require it. For example, if a person who is used to drinking alcohol embraces Islam, their mentor, or someone who has authority, should tell them that they must remove from their home and workplace anything that is specifically related to drinking alcohol, such as wine glasses. If the person has a small bar, they should remove it. They should remove also any brewing facilities they

7. Ibn Ḥibbān, *Ṣaḥīḥ*, vol. 12, p. 221.
8. Ibn Mājah, *Sunan*, vol. 2, p. 1128.

have. Needless to say, glasses, shelves, bars and brewing facilities do not [in themselves] make anything unlawful, but the ruling that applies to them is that they are prohibited in that person's particular case; but God knows best. We may expand this so as to conclude that a Muslim ruler may legislate to forbid people anything that leads to the contravention of religious rules and edicts, and he may bind them to observe such prohibitions, even if there is no explicit text to apply in such cases.

The third part of the Hadith concerns the visiting of graves. In its different versions, the Hadith says: 'So visit them [i.e. graves] but do not say vulgar words'[9] and 'So visit them and let your visit increase you in goodness.'[10] A different version is: 'So visit them, because visiting graves softens hearts, makes the eyes tearful and reminds you of the Day of Judgement. Do not say vulgar words.'[11] Commenting on this Hadith, al-Bayḍāwī said: 'The Prophet meant that his earlier prohibition was to stop them from doing as people did in pre-Islamic days when they boasted about numbers. Now that Islam had destroyed the very foundations of idolatry, visiting graves was recommended because such visits soften the visitors' hearts and remind them of death.'[12] This reason is not specifically mentioned, but it is deduced from the way the Hadith is worded and it is confirmed by the well-known practices of the Arabs in pre-Islamic days, as they used to boast about their glorious days at graveyards. Ibn 'Abbās said: 'surah 102 was revealed concerning two clans of the Quraysh, the 'Abd Manāf and Sahm clans. In

9. Mālik, *al-Muwaṭṭa'*, vol. 6, p. 373.
10. Al-Ḥākim al-Naysābūrī, *al-Mustadrak 'alā al-Ṣaḥīḥayn*, vol. 4, p. 232.
11. Ibid., vol. 1, p. 532.
12. Al-Zurqānī, *Sharḥ al-Zurqānī 'alā al-Muwaṭṭa'*, vol. 3, p. 101.

their mutual antagonism they extolled the praises of their chiefs and dignitaries in [the age of] Islam. Each clan said: "We have more honourable people, and our chiefs are more respected, we are larger in number and our help is sought." The 'Abd Manāf scored higher. Then they boasted about their dead, and the Sahm scored higher. God then revealed the surah beginning: "*You are so preoccupied with boasting about numbers that you even visit graveyards*", *taking pride in your dead ancestors*.'[13] (102: 1–2)

Ibn Buraydah said about this surah: 'It was revealed concerning two rival clans of the Anṣār. They said to each other: "Have you anyone like our so-and-so?" The others replied with the same. They were all praising their living people. They then said: "Let us now go to the graveyard." One clan would point to a grave and ask the other: "Have you anyone like so-and-so?" The others said the same. God then revealed the surah saying: "*You are so preoccupied with boasting about numbers that you would even visit graveyards*."'[14] (102: 1–2)

We see how Arab tribes in Makkah and Yathrib (later Madīnah) would boast about their honourable people to the extent that they would go to graveyards to point at certain graves of their ancestors and praise them, instead of thinking about death and heeding its lessons. It is certainly possible that the objective of the Prophet's initial prohibition was to stop such vulgarity. Once the trivialities of pre-Islamic days were consigned to oblivion, he reverted to the original ruling that the visiting of graves was permissible. He added some recommendations to observe when making such visits. Visitors must not say anything vulgar, in order to guard against reverting to such unbecoming practices.

---

13. Al-Qurṭubī, *Tafsīr*.
14. Ibn Kathīr, *Tafsīr*.

The initial order prohibiting visiting graveyards remains appropriate in certain communities of unbelievers in different parts of the world where people continue to observe some strange practices. Many non-Muslim communities make graves like idols which they worship, and they may commit gross indecencies at graveyards. Should any such community embrace Islam, their teachers should order them not to visit graveyards until Islam is well established in their hearts and minds, and all traces of ignorance and idolatry have been purged from their community. We see here some similarities with the prohibition of brewing drinks in certain containers as a training method based on removing what facilitates sin. All three subjects mentioned in the Hadith confirm that the ruler of a Muslim community should take measures that help to safeguard the essentials outlined by Islam. One of these is to safeguard religion: that is, the true and pure faith. This was the objective in this particular case.

There are many other examples of issues that are subject to claimed abrogation, despite the fact that the earlier or later rulings have clear reasons which are easily understood from the viewpoint of the objectives of Islamic law and the role of the ruler in its enforcement.

For example, God says: '*Say: "In all that has been revealed to me, I do not find anything forbidden to eat, if one wishes to eat thereof, unless it be carrion, or blood poured forth, or the flesh of swine – for all that is unclean – or a sinful offering over which any name other than God's has been invoked. But if one is driven by necessity, neither intending disobedience nor exceeding his bare need, then know that your Lord is much-forgiving, ever merciful.*"' (6: 145) In reference to this Qur'ānic verse, al-Shāfi'ī observed: 'Ibn 'Abbās, 'Ā'ishah and 'Ubayd ibn 'Umayr said that there is nothing to prevent one eating anything other than what God has forbidden. Their argument relies on the Qur'ān. These people were of the highest calibre in knowledge and piety.'[15] However, the majority of scholars claim that the meaning of the above-mentioned verse is narrowed down by the Hadiths that prohibit eating the flesh of domestic donkeys. Some of them claim that these Hadiths abrogate this Qur'ānic verse.[16]

Both al-Bukhārī and Muslim relate in their *Ṣaḥīḥ* anthologies certain Hadiths narrated by Ibn 'Umar, 'Alī, al-Barā' ibn 'Āzib and Ibn Abī Awfā stating that the Prophet (peace be upon him) prohibited eating the flesh of domestic donkeys at the time of the Battle of Khaybar.[17] Ibn al-'Arabī and other scholars reject the claim of abrogation as they attach the Prophet's prohibition to a particular reason. Ibn al-'Arabī summarises the different views expressed by scholars, saying that they attribute the prohibition to one of three reasons: (i) they were cooked before the division of war gains; (ii) these particular animals fed on animal faeces; or (iii) a man came to the Prophet complaining, 'Donkeys have almost died out! Donkeys have almost died out!' Therefore, the Prophet stood up and announced the prohibition of eating their meat because of the danger that they would all be killed. Ibn al-'Arabī comments on the last reason that if they are plentiful and using them for food will not cause difficulties in carrying travellers' baggage, eating them becomes permissible. A ruling is waived if the reason for it is removed.[18] These reasons for the prohibition mentioned by Ibn al-'Arabī are stated in the following narrations.

---

15. Al-Shāfi'ī, *al-Umm*, vol. 4, p. 151.
16. Ibn al-'Arabī, *Aḥkām al-Qur'ān*, vol. 2, p. 291.
17. Al-Bukhārī, *Ṣaḥīḥ*, vol. 5, pp. 2012, 2502; Muslim, Ṣaḥīḥ, vol. 6, p. 63.
18. Ibn al-'Arabī, *Aḥkām al-Qur'ān*, vol. 2, p. 292.

Al-Bukhārī related on the authority of Ibn Abī Awfā: 'One day at the time of Khaybar we were hungry. Large saucepans were boiling and some were practically cooked. A messenger from the Prophet came over and said: "Do not eat any donkey meat. Throw it away".' Ibn Abī Awfa said: 'We discussed the matter and some suggested that he had prohibited eating them because they were war gains that had not been divided. Some said that he made such a total prohibition because they were animals that ate faeces.'[19]

Another version is also related by al-Bukhārī on the authority of Anas ibn Mālik: 'A man came to God's Messenger (peace be upon him) and said: "Donkeys have been eaten up." Then another man came and said: "Donkeys have died out." He ordered someone to announce to the people: "God and His Messenger forbid you to eat the meat of domestic donkeys, because they are abominable." Saucepans were poured out as they were boiling with meat.'[20]

Abū Dāwūd's version is narrated by Ghālib ibn Abjar: 'We were going through a period of drought and I had nothing to feed my family except some donkey meat, but God's Messenger had prohibited the meat of domestic donkeys. I went to the Prophet and said: "Messenger of God, we are going through this drought and I have nothing to feed my family except some fat donkeys, but you have prohibited the meat of domestic donkeys." He said: "Feed your family with your fat donkeys. I only forbade it earlier because in that town they ate faeces."'[21] Although this Hadith related by Abū Dāwūd gives a clear reason for the prohibition, its

19. Al-Bukhārī, *Ṣaḥīḥ*, vol. 4, p. 1545.
20. Ibid., vol. 5, p. 2103; Ibn Ḥibbān, *Ṣaḥīḥ*.
21. Abū Dāwūd, *Sunan*, vol. 3, p. 356. Abū Dāwūd points out that questions were raised concerning the transmission of this Hadith.

chain of transmission has been questioned. However, it is supported by a different version narrated by Umm Naṣr of Muḥārib. She said: 'A man asked the Messenger of God (peace be upon him) about the meat of domestic donkeys. The Prophet asked him: "Do they not feed on grass and tree leaves?" The man replied that they did. The Prophet said: "Then you may eat of their meat."'[22]

Al-Bukhārī's second narration suggests that the reason for the prohibition was the small number of donkeys that were available as mounts, which is confirmed by Ibn 'Abbās. Despite the questions raised about their chains of transmission, the two versions given by Abū Dāwūd confirm that donkey meat is not absolutely forbidden to eat, but the reason for the prohibition was that those particular donkeys fed on faeces. According to one narration by al-Bukhārī, some of the Prophet's Companions shared this view. Both suggested reasons are strengthened by the fact that the Prophet permitted eating the meat of the zebra, which in Arabic is called a 'wild donkey'.[23] There is not much difference between the two species, apart from their

---

22. Al-Ṭabarānī, *al-Mu'jam al-Awsaṭ*, vol. 5, p. 198 and *al-Mu'jam al-Kabīr*, vol. 25, p. 161. See also Ibn Abī Ḥātim, *al-Jarḥ wa al-Ta'dīl*, vol. 2, p. 138; al-Ḥāzimī, *al-I'tibār fī al-Nāsikh wa al-Mansūkh fī al-Ḥadīth*, vol. 1, p. 59.
23. Muslim, *Ṣaḥīḥ*, chapter on the prohibition of hunting while in the state of consecration (*iḥrām*). Abū Qatādah reports that he was with God's Messenger (peace be upon him). 'On their way towards Makkah, he stayed behind with some friends who were in the state of consecration, but he was not. He saw a zebra, and he jumped on his horse. He asked his friends to hand him his whip, but they refused. He asked them to give him his spear, and they refused. He took it himself and chased the zebra and killed it. Some of the Prophet's Companions ate of its meat while others did not. When they caught up with the Prophet, they asked him about its meat. He said: "It is a meal God has given you."'

respective names and the colour of their skin. There is no substantial difference between them from the Islamic point of view. It is possible that the initial prohibition was for both reasons, which makes the overall objective of the prohibition the preservation of Muslim life through the availability of sufficient mounts and the prevention of eating polluted meat.

In the light of the foregoing, the Prophet's actions in political, economic, educational, military and health matters differed according to the circumstances he faced at different stages of his mission. Hence they may be transmitted to us in the form of an 'initial permission followed by prohibition' or an 'initial prohibition, later relaxed'. We should understand all these as falling within the one framework of the objectives of leadership to safeguard people's faith, property, life, and so on. We should not go into claiming abrogation based on personal opinion. In this way, we will be able to understand the Prophet's Sunnah and implement it in these public areas according to their meanings and objectives, not merely according to their words and forms.

2. The objective of making things easier through gradual implementation of Islamic laws

It is part of human nature that changing habits is difficult. Prior to Islam, Arabs acquired habits and traditions that became essential aspects of their life. Islam established certain manners, values and rulings that were contrary to such habits and traditions. However, it was by God's grace and the Prophet's wisdom that the implementation of Islamic rules took a gradual approach, which became one of the main features of the Islamic message during the Prophet's lifetime.

This gradual approach moved in two ways. One was to start with a lighter command before gradually making it harder and harder; and the other was to start with a rigorous command, then make it gradually lighter and lighter. Examples of the first way include the prohibition of alcohol and usury, both of which started with partial denunciation and ended with complete prohibition. In the case of prayer, it started as twice a day and ended as five times daily, while fasting was initially required for a few days only and was increased to the duty to fast throughout the month of Ramadan. Initially Muslims could speak during prayer, but ordinary speech while praying was later forbidden.

In the case of alcohol, God first revealed the verse that says: '*They ask you about intoxicants and games of chance. Say, "In both there is great evil although they have some benefits for people, but their evil is far greater than their benefit.*"' (2: 219) This is a clear reference to the principle that if something involves more evil than good, it should be given up. Later, another verse told Muslims: '*Believers, do not attempt to pray when you are drunk, [but wait] until you know what you are saying.*' (4: 43) This meant that people could not drink throughout the day and part of the night. Finally, the total prohibition, which is the originally intended ruling, was imposed in the verse that says: '*O you who believe, intoxicants, games of chance, idolatrous practices and divining arrows are abominations devised by Satan; therefore, avoid them so that you may be successful.*' (5: 90)

There were similar stages in the prohibition of all usury. It started with the verse: '*Whatever you give out in usury so that it may increase through other people's property will bring no increase from God.*' (30: 39) This is an admonition in negative form, stating that usury earns no reward with

God. Later, the Qur'ān mentioned the case of the Jews who were punished by God for gorging themselves on usury even though God made it forbidden for them. God then ordered Muslims: '*Believers, do not gorge yourselves on usury, doubling [your money] again and again.*' (3: 130) This was a prohibition of high rates of usury, which could double the lender's money. Finally, God told Muslims: '*Believers, fear God and give up what remains outstanding of usury gains, if you are true believers.*' (2: 278) This makes clear that all types and all rates of usury are completely forbidden. This is the originally intended ruling.

Prayer was originally required to be offered from time to time. After a while it became a duty as two *rak'ah*s in the morning and two in the evening. Finally, the five daily prayers were made obligatory during the Prophet's night journey.[24]

Fasting is another example of the gradual approach in arriving at the final duty. Mu'ādh ibn Jabal narrates: 'When God's Messenger migrated to Madīnah, he fasted on the tenth day of Muḥarram and three days each month. God subsequently made fasting during the month of Ramadan obligatory. God, the Exalted, revealed: "*Believers, fasting is decreed for you as it was decreed for those before you, so that you may be God-fearing. [Fast] on a certain number of days. But whoever of you is ill or on a journey may instead fast the same number of days later on. Those who find fasting a strain too hard to bear may compensate for it by feeding a needy person.*"' (2: 183–4) The rule that prevailed then was that a person may choose to fast or to feed a needy person instead. Then God made it obligatory to fast for everyone who was healthy and not travelling. The option of feeding a

24. Abū Bakr al-Dimyāṭī, *I'ānat al-Ṭālibīn*, vol. 1, p. 21.

needy person remains available to elderly persons who find fasting too hard.

Examples of the second way, which is to start with the hard duty before reducing it, include the requirement of standing up in night worship, and continuing to fast for the second day if a person falls asleep before ending their fast. The first was reduced so as to make night worship recommended, not obligatory, while the second made fasting two days together clearly discouraged.

On the case of continuing to fast for a second day, al-Barā' reports: 'It was required of the Companions that if one was fasting and it was time to end one's fast, but one slept before eating, one could not eat for the rest of the night and the following day until the evening. It happened that Qays ibn Saramah al-Anṣārī was fasting, and when it was time to end his fast he went home. He asked his wife: "Do you have anything to eat?" She said: "No, but I will go and fetch you something." He had been working all day, and he fell asleep. When his wife came back and saw him [asleep], she said: "Poor man!" When it was midday the following day, he fell unconscious. The Prophet was told, and then God revealed the verse: "*It is lawful for you to be intimate with your wives during the night preceding the fast... Eat and drink until you can see the white streak of dawn against the blackness of the night.*" (2: 187) They were exceedingly delighted with it.'[25]

On the matter of night worship, Sa'd ibn Hishām reports: 'I said to 'Ā'ishah: "Tell me about the night worship of the Messenger of God." She said: "When it was revealed to him: '*You enfolded one, stand in prayer at night, all but a small part of it*' (73: 1–2), they [meaning he and his Companions] offered night worship for a year, until their

25. Al-Tirmidhī, *Sunan*, vol. 5, p. 201.

feet were swollen. Then God revealed the verse that says: '*Recite of the Qur'ān as much as may be easy for you. He knows that some of you will be sick.*'"'[26] (73: 20)

The objective of the first way of starting with the easier duty before increasing it was to allow human nature to do its work as people would get used to the lighter duty. When natural resistance was overcome, the full duty outlined in the originally intended ruling would be required. The objective of the second way, starting with the harder duty before reducing it, was to train people to undertake the hard task right at the beginning so that they would acquire certain habits. Later, the duty was reduced to make only recommended what was previously compulsory.

It is the usual practice to include rulings that were arrived at gradually under the heading of 'abrogation'. For example, it is said that the verse that prohibited alcoholic drinks abrogated the one that told Muslims not to offer prayers when they were under the influence of alcoholic drink. It is also said that the verse that told Muslims to recite in their night worship whatever was easy for them abrogated the one that ordered them to stand up in prayer at night. Furthermore, it is claimed that the ruling prohibiting ordinary speech during prayer abrogated the permission to speak while praying. This is claimed although the religious ruling on each of these questions is one, which is the final ruling. Although we may have any agreed terminology, I am reluctant to include such a gradual approach under 'abrogation', because it is problematic on two counts.

Firstly, to say that the gradual stages represent 'religious rulings' even though they are described as 'abrogated' is rather inaccurate. There was never a religious ruling

26. Al-Ḥākim al-Naysābūrī, *al-Mustadrak*, vol. 2, p. 548.

permitting drinking alcohol at night or another permitting usury that does not double the lender's money. The ruling concerning alcoholic drinks, and the one concerning usury, were always the same in the Divine faith, which is total and absolute prohibition, but the implementation of this ruling was gradual.

Secondly, when we say that the different stages of gradual implementation represent abrogated rulings, we suggest that these interim rulings may not be applied at any time. However, a careful reading of the Prophet's Hadiths gives a different conclusion.

In all cases of gradual implementation we find one or more narrations indicating that the later ruling remained as final and applicable, but the earlier ruling remained valid in special cases, or as a concession, because it is the lighter ruling which was replaced by a harder one. To give a few examples: speaking or turning one's face during prayer remains acceptable in cases of necessity. The Prophet (peace be upon him) allowed some newcomers to Islam to offer two prayers a day instead of five so that they could become used to prayer. Drinking a small amount of alcohol is permissible for one who could die of thirst and there is nothing else to drink. By analogy, a little drink may be permissible to an alcoholic while he is going through a rehabilitation treatment. Similar cases may apply.

A Hadith related by Abū Dāwūd from 'Abd Allāh ibn Fuḍālah from his father says: 'God's Messenger (peace be upon him) taught me, and in his teaching he told me: "Attend regularly to the five obligatory prayers." I said: "During these times I am often preoccupied. Give me something comprehensive which will discharge my duty if I observe it." He said: "Then be sure to offer the two *'aṣrs*." This word was unfamiliar to us, so I asked: "What are the two *'aṣrs*?" He said: "A prayer before sunrise and a prayer before sunset."'[27] In his *Musnad* Aḥmad relates a similar Hadith. In his book *al-Fatḥ al-Rabbānī*, which is a highly useful rearrangement of *al-Musnad* with brief comments and explanations, Shaykh Aḥmad 'Abd al-Raḥmān al-Sā'atī includes this Hadith in a chapter with the heading: 'Encouraging unbelievers to accept Islam and winning their hearts.'[28] The same idea is expressed in a Hadith related by Abū Dāwūd quoting Wahb: 'I asked Jābir about the case of [the newly Muslim tribe of] Thaqīf. He said: "They stipulated a condition that they pay no Zakat and do not take part in *jihād*. But he heard the Prophet say afterwards: 'They shall pay Zakat and shall take part in *jihād*.'"'[29]

Study of the Sunnah shows that the harder ruling that was given initially as training and education for the Companions, but was later replaced by a lighter ruling, was not completely annulled. It remains applicable as a method of hard training. Examples include night worship, fasting on the tenth of Muḥarram, fasting three days a month, and the breaking of utensils used to brew alcoholic drinks. Abū Dāwūd relates Abū Hurayrah's narration: 'My close friend (peace be upon him) urged me to do three things and I never neglect them even when I travel. They are: offering two voluntary *rak'ah*s mid-morning, fasting three days a month and not going to sleep without praying the *Witr*.'[30]

In any case, everyone must realise that God's ruling on any of these cases is the one ruling. The gradual strengthening or lightening of the ruling only represents stages in the

27. It is also narrated in al-Ḥākim al-Naysābūrī, *al-Mustadrak*, vol. 1, p. 70.
28. Quoted from 'Abd al-Jalīl 'Īsā, *Ijtihād al-Rasūl*, p. 122.
29. Abū Dāwūd, *Sunan*, vol. 3, p. 163.
30. Ibid., vol. 2, p. 65.

Islamic process of education of Muslim individuals and communities.

Shaykh Muḥammad al-Ghazālī (may God bestow mercy on him) commented on what he called 'the conceived contradiction' in the concept of abrogation. He said: 'The various items of legislation concerning a particular issue are carefully arranged, so that each Qur'ānic verse operates within its defined scope. If that scope is completed and replaced by another, a different verse deals with it giving a new directive. Is it right to call such gradual legislation an abrogation? Medicines remain necessary as long as the relevant diseases remain. A particular medicine may treat a particular case, but may not even be considered in the treatment of another. Yet this does not detract from the value of such a medicine. Indeed, the same illness may require a sequence of medications, each suiting a particular stage of the disease, its complications, and its aftermath... The verses of the Qur'ān are very much similar to this. Hence, we wonder at the great usage of abrogation by commentators.'[31]

3. Striking the balance between the objectives of worship and keeping things easy

Scholars have different views about whether a traveller in Ramadan should fast or not. There are Hadiths which appear superficially contradictory, as they state that on certain occasions God's messenger (peace be upon him) observed the fast when travelling but he did not fast on other occasions. Muslim enters in his *Ṣaḥīḥ* a narration by Ibn 'Abbās saying: 'Do not criticise anyone who fasts or anyone who does not. God's Messenger fasted on some journeys

31. Muḥammad al-Ghazālī, *Naẓarāt fī al-Qur'ān*, p. 194.

and did not fast on others.'[32] Muslim also relates in his *Ṣaḥīḥ* a Hadith narrated by Ibn 'Abbās saying: 'God's Messenger started his journey during the Year of the Conquest in Ramadan. He fasted until he reached al-Kudayd, but he did not fast after that.'[33]

Commenting on this Hadith, Ibn Shihāb al-Zuhrī holds – as Muslim reports – that the ruling that permits fasting during travel is 'abrogated', because the narration stating that the Prophet (peace be upon him) did not fast on this journey was the later practice. It was in the year that Makkah fell to Islam. Ibn Shihāb said: 'Not fasting was the last practice, and we take the Prophet's latest action… His Companions used always to follow the latest, considering it to be definitive and abrogating any earlier ruling.'[34]

However, Muslim also includes a Hadith which combines the two options in a better way than keeping the choice open as Ibn 'Abbās's narration suggests. Abū Sa'īd al-Khudrī reports: 'We used to go on expeditions in Ramaḍān with God's Messenger (peace be upon him). Some of us would be fasting and some would not. None who fasted blamed any who did not fast, and those who were not fasting did not blame those who fasted. They all considered that the one who felt himself strong enough to fast did well and the one who did not fast, feeling his lack of strength, did well.'[35] This view links worship to the status of the individual. For the one who feels himself strong keeping up the worship is better, while the easier option of not fasting is better for the one who felt himself not strong enough. Striking the balance between the two objectives of attending to worship and

32. Muslim, *Ṣaḥīḥ*, vol. 2, p. 789.
33. Ibid., vol. 2, p. 785.
34. Ibid.
35. Ibid., pp. 786–7.

opting for what is easy is an essential feature of Islamic law. When hard acts of worship become too hard for a person, a concession is always given, within the framework of Islamic law.

4. Balancing the objectives of human beings' safety and protecting the environment

We may look at another case of striking a balance between the objectives of Islamic law. Again, we find different views suggesting abrogation or preference in this case, while looking at the objectives enables us to put the different options within the same framework of ensuring the safety of human beings and their environment. In his *Ṣaḥīḥ*, Muslim includes a chapter with the heading: 'The order to kill dogs, and its abrogation, and the prohibition of owning a dog except for hunting, or a farm dog or a sheep dog, and so on.' In this chapter Muslim mentions: 'Ibn 'Umar reports that God's Messenger (peace be upon him) ordered the killing of dogs, except a hunting dog, or a sheep or cattle dog.'[36] Another Hadith on the same topic is considered by scholars to abrogate the earlier Hadith: 'Had it not been that dogs are a community like all others, I would have ordered their killing. Kill of them only those which are completely black.'[37]

Some scholars have taken the first Hadith as giving an absolute religious order, and that it was subsequently abrogated so that only black dogs could be killed. This is the apparent meaning of the second, abrogating Hadith. Other scholars do not consider the first order to be abrogated,

36. Ibid., vol. 3, p. 1200.
37. Abū Dāwūd, *Sunan*, vol. 3, p. 108. A similar Hadith is related in Aḥmad, *Musnad*, pp. 20, 590.

but they suggest that it is left to the ruler's discretion. Ibn Wahb said: 'I heard Mālik say about the killing of dogs: "I do not see any wrong if the ruler orders their killing."' This means that Mālik feels that it is determined by the ruler as he considers what serves public interests. This is fine, as it allows both Hadiths to be enforced.

Al-Qurṭubī expresses a similar opinion: 'What is understood from these Hadiths is that the killing of dogs, apart from the excepted ones, is required if they cause harm to the Muslim community. If the harm is extensive, this order becomes a duty. If it is rare, then the duty is to kill those dogs which are harmful.'[38] Ibn Rushd said: 'Many scholars are of the view that no dog, black or of other colours, should be killed, except an aggressive biting dog… They base their view on the Hadith which mentions that a man saw a dog panting of thirst, and he went into a well, brought up water and gave some to the dog to drink. God thanked him and forgave him his sins. God's Messenger said: "Any kindness to a moist-livered creature earns a reward from God." These scholars said: if kindness to such an animal earns a reward, then harming it incurs a sin. There can be no greater harm than killing such an animal.'[39]

If we consider the objectives of Islamic law, we do not see this as an issue of worship in any way. The explanation of contradictory texts is based on balancing two clear interests: that of human beings and that of animals, or in our modern parlance, human health and a healthy environment. It appears that the first Hadith, ordering the killing of dogs, was said at a time when wild dogs represented a danger to the population of Madīnah. Hence, the Prophet issued this

38. Muḥammad ibn Muḥammad al-Maghribī, *Mawāhib al-Jalīl li-Sharḥ Mukhtaṣar Khalīl*, vol. 3, p. 236.
39. Ibid., quoting Ibn Rushd, vol. 3, p. 237.

order. This was not a religious ruling, but a protective health measure. The second Hadith was at a later date, when dogs did not represent any danger to people. The Prophet (peace be upon him) wanted to teach us that animal communities, which the Qur'ān describes as similar to our human community, have the right to exist, unless they represent a serious danger to human beings.

The right view in questions of the environment generally is the middle one between two extremes: one prohibits whatever harms the natural environment in any way, even if this causes harm to human beings. This is what is advocated by 'Green' parties and those who advocate the creation of protected natural areas in the present time. The opposite view shows no respect to any creatures but human beings and cares nothing if an action leads to some species becoming extinct. The two superficially contradictory Hadiths we have quoted teach humankind a lesson in the need to strike the right balance between the safety of human beings and the safety of the environment. To conclude: this chapter, which merely gives some examples, illustrates that looking at and implementing the objectives of texts allows Islamic *fiqh* to address the problems of the age and enables it to retain its flexibility so that it can deal with whatever people may need in their daily life.

Theoretical and Practical Conclusions

IN THE light of this discussion we arrive at the conclusion that Islamic rulings must be based on understanding the objectives behind religious texts, rather than understanding the meanings of individual words and expressions. If we limit ourselves to the meanings of individual words, which may be mutually contradictory with regard to time, place, situation, persons, intentions or effects, without looking at their higher concepts which are not confined to time and place and are not related to particular persons or cultures, we will inevitably arrive at unfounded simplistic dualisms. It is such dualisms that have led to thousands of conceived cases of contradictions, such as those mentioned in this book. Such dualisms have, over many centuries and in our own time, restricted the ability of Islamic *fiqh* to renew itself so as to meet the needs of changing circumstances in order to fulfil its essential objectives and achieve its noble aims.

Therefore, we require the learned mind to abandon the theory of abrogation as a means of reconciling assumed verbal contradictions – apart from the fact that Islam has abrogated earlier codes of law, and the abrogation that is within the gradual approach to problems prior to arriving at final rulings. It is imperative that the scholarly intellect be allowed to explore the broader objectives so as to implement all texts that have the same aims even though they have different wordings.

Based on this theoretical conclusion and how we have dealt with the examples cited in this book, we may briefly state the following thirty practical conclusions.The objective of Zakat is to take a portion of the property of people who have more than the minimum amount of wealth and give it to others who are poor and needy, regardless of the types and types of wealth. The amounts and rates established by Islam must be implemented, but not the other details that are not affected by the laws and regulations of Zakat. All claims of abrogation suggested in this area are to be discounted.

- The objective of requiring a man who divorces his wife by choice to pay her maintenance is that he should bear some financial responsibility towards his former wife whom he chose to leave, regardless of the philosophical disagreement concerned with the concept of opposite implications, and regardless of the imaginary claims of abrogation in this connection.

- It is imperative that a Muslim prioritises legitimate interests at the individual and community levels. Top priority should be given to safeguarding the essentials (*ḍarūrāt*), namely faith, life, mind, offspring, honour and property. Next on the list of priorities is the safeguarding of needs (*ḥājiyyāt*), such as marriage, business and consumer goods. Then he must look to safeguard enhancements (*taḥsīniyyāt*), such as goods that one can do without. This order of priorities should be considered in the allocation of effort, time and available resources.

- It is imperative that Muslims seek out the essential points and the wisdom behind the Islamic beliefs in God, His Books and Messengers, the Day of Judgement, Divine Will, and God's attributes and actions. Muslims must also keep such wisdom and objectives in mind in their dealings with God and with people.

- The advocacy of Islam must be based on the objectives of Islam, particularly in countries with Muslim minorities. Thus, Islam should be presented through its aims and objectives, rather than its rulings on different issues. This is the approach that comes closer to the rational method, which is widely followed in our present time.

- Islam rejects all bad omens, particularly in relation to women. To associate women with bad omens and to treat them as inferior beings are practices of the people of ignorance which Islam rejects. Hadiths and scholars' arguments that are contrary to this principle are unauthentic, even if they are found in authentic Hadith collections.

- Narrations and fatwas about 'equal standing' in marriage have no authentic basis. The underlying principle in this regard is the Hadith 'If a man whose level of faith and manners are acceptable comes to you with a proposal of marriage, accept his proposal.' Women may follow funeral processions, and they may recite the Qur'ān at any time. Hadiths and arguments by scholars to the contrary cannot be right.

- None of the religious texts that give women all their social and political rights and full legal jurisdiction over their affairs have been abrogated, although some of these texts are contrary to some traditions that prevail in communities that treat women as inferior beings, or are contrary to some scholars' preconceived ideas.

- The essential ruling concerning meat is that all meat is permissible to eat except what the Qur'ān specifies to be unlawful. Hadiths and scholarly views contrary to this cannot be true.

- It is certainly incorrect to claim that some verses of the Qur'ān were abrogated in written form, which means that they were removed after they had been written in scrolls. The Qur'ān is preserved intact by God, Who revealed it, and no change or alteration may creep into it in any way.

- There is no contradiction, mutual exclusion or abrogation concerning Zakat, voluntary charity (*ṣadaqah*), the maintenance of one's family or relatives, and similar matters. All these are important aspects of Islamic law.

- The claim that the prohibition of fighting in the sacred months has been abrogated cannot be proven, apart from the exception, clearly stated in the Qur'ān, relating to self-defence.

- Making financial compensation for not fasting in Ramadan remains applicable to individuals who find fasting too hard. This is not abrogated or annulled. It remains valid for elderly men and women and similar persons. These people may feed a poor person for every day they do not fast.

- Fasting is the preferred option for a person who is able to fast when travelling in Ramaḍān. If Muslims feel too weak they are allowed not to fast during travel.

- The verses detailing the shares of inheritance have not abrogated making bequests by will, even to close relatives or to heirs. Such bequests by will may be made in favour of relatives who are not heirs and to heirs with special circumstances that necessitate giving them more than their apportioned shares. The Hadith that says: 'No will may be made in favour of an heir' is questionable in some ways. Moreover, a Hadith may not abrogate or be in contradiction with a text of the Qur'ān.

- To wipe over one's *khuffs*, or leather socks, as a substitute for washing one's feet continues to be valid as part of ablution. Its abrogation, or annulment, was merely imagined by some of the Prophet's Companions. No religious ruling ever abrogated it.

- The hide of a dead animal is considered cleansed when tanned. That this ruling was abrogated or annulled was merely imagined by some scholars. No religious ruling ever abrogated it.

- If the division of the estate of a deceased person is attended by relatives, orphans and needy people, then they should be given a small portion of the estate and should be spoken to kindly. That this was abrogated or annulled was merely imagined by some of the Prophet's Companions. It was never a religious ruling.

- The prohibition to marry an adulterous woman remains in force, unless she repents. The abrogation or annulment of this ruling was not a new religious ruling; rather, it was a mistaken view of some scholars (may God bestow mercy on them).

- The Qur'ānic verses that call for pardon, forgiveness, leniency, patience, honouring promises and pledges, good neighbourliness, freedom of belief, dialogue and coexistence are all clear and definitive. There is no contradiction between these verses and the one called the 'Verse of the Sword'.

- The concession that allows a Muslim state not to undertake legitimate jihad when it is in a state of weakness that puts it in a perilous situation is not contrary to its duty of jihad when it is in a state of strength. This is an area that is subject to wise political decisions.

- If an offender declares their repentance and this is openly confirmed, such repentance must be accepted, even if the offence is one that carries a mandatory punishment (*ḥadd*). The repentance waives only the punishment that pertains to the rights due to God. The rights of other people must be exacted in full. This is a better way of combating crime, reforming offenders and keeping society on the right course than enforcing punishment.

- Although the majority of scholars continue to uphold stoning as the mandatory punishment for married adulterers, consistency with the true spirit of Islam supports the view that stoning was a punishment prescribed in the Jewish code of law. It was abrogated by Islam as defined by the Qur'ānic verse stating flogging as the punishment for adultery.

- The overall objective of the Hadiths speaking about the meat of sacrifice suggests that the ruler has a duty to take measures to ensure the protection of the main life essentials, such as protecting people from hunger, and promoting mutual social solidarity (*takāful*) within the Muslim community. This is to be balanced against the fact that Islam allows free personal ownership and allows the use of what one owns, as long as the community as a whole is not in need of such resources.

- Muftis may prohibit visiting graves in cases where Islamic values have not yet taken hold in people's hearts and minds. They may issue such a fatwa to stop practices that are contrary to Islam. This is done owing to the need to close the means to indulge in sin, which is not subject to abrogation.

- If a person who habitually drinks alcohol embraces Islam, their imam should tell them that it is their duty to remove from their home and workplace anything specifically related to drinking, such as wine glasses, wine shelves, special containers, and so on, because in this Muslim's particular case these are closely related to drinking what is forbidden.

- A gradual approach to the implementation of Islamic rulings is a confirmed Sunnah, particularly in the case of a new Muslim who is unfamiliar with Islamic values and practices.

- In cases of gradual implementation, interim rulings that were applied during the Prophet's lifetime remain valid and may be upheld in special cases or as a concession. Examples of such interim rulings include turning or speaking during prayer when that is very necessary, and the permission given by the Prophet to new Muslims to offer two prayers instead of the obligatory five until they get used to prayer. Another example is to allow a person who is almost dying of thirst to take a small measure of an alcoholic drink if it is the only drink available. By analogy, a drug addict may be allowed a small dose during the treatment and rehabilitation period. Other areas may be determined on the basis of analogy.

- Islam strikes a balance between the welfare of human beings and animal welfare, as well as between people's health and a healthy environment. What is right in cases affecting the environment generally is the middle course between two extremes: between the one that wants to outlaw everything that affects the environment, even though it may cause harm to people and human habitat, and the other which cares for nothing except human beings, even if this means the extinction of some species. The objective of Islamic law is to maintain balance in all fields.

In conclusion, I praise God, the Lord of all Worlds. May He bestow His blessings on Muḥammad, who was His last Messenger to mankind.

Bibliography

'Abdu, Muḥammad. *Tafsīr al-Qur'ān al-Ḥakīm*.

Abū Dāwūd, Sulaymān ibn al-Ash'ath. *Sunan Abī Dāwūd*. Ed. Muḥammad Muḥyī al-Dīn 'Abd al-Ḥamīd. Beirut: Dār al-Fikr, n.d.

Abū al-Maḥāsin, Yūsuf ibn Mūsā. *Mu'tasar al-Mukhtaṣar*. Cairo, Maktabat Beirut; Beirut: 'Ālam al-Kutub, n.d.

Abū Shuqqah, 'Abd al-Ḥalīm. *Taḥrīr al-Mar'ah fī 'aṣr al-Risālah*. 4th ed. Kuwait and Cairo: Dār al-Qalam, 1995.

Abū Zuhrah, Muḥammad. *Uṣūl al-Fiqh*. Cairo: Dār al-Fikr al-'Arabī, 1997.

Al-Alwānī, Ṭāhā Jābir. *Maqāṣid al-Sharī'ah*. Beirut: Dār al-Hādī, 2001.

Al-Āmidī, 'Alī ibn Muḥammad. *al-Aḥkām*. Ed. Sayyid al-Jumaylī. Beirut: Dār al-Kitāb al-'Arabī, 1984.

Audah, 'Abd al-Qādir. *al-Mawsū'ah al-'aṣriyyah fī al-Fiqh al-Jinā'ī al-Islāmī*. Cairo: Dār al-Shurūq, 2001.

Audah, ʿAbd al-Qādir. *al-Tashrīʿ al-Jināʾī al-Islāmī*. 10th ed. Cairo: Muʾassasat al-Risālah, 1989.

Al-Awa, Muḥammad Saleem. *Fī Uṣūl al-Niẓām al-Jināʾī al-Islāmī*. Cairo: Dār Naḥḍat Miṣr, 2006.

Al-Awa, Muḥammad Saleem et al. *al-Sunnah al-Tashrīʿiyyah wa Ghayr al-Tashrīʿiyyah*. Cairo: Dār Nahdat Miṣr, 2001.

Al-ʿAẓīm-Ābādī, Muḥammad Shams al-Ḥaqq. *ʿAwn al-Maʿbūd*. 2nd ed. Beirut: Dār al-Kutub al-ʿIlmiyyah, 1995.

Badrān, Badrān Abū al-ʿAynayn. *Adillat al-Tashrīʿ al-Mutaʿāriḍah wa Wujūh al-Tarjīḥ Baynahā*. Alexandria: Muʾassasat Shabāb al-Jāmiʿah, 1974.

Al-Barakātī, Muḥammad ʿAmīm al-Iḥsān al-Mujaddidī. *Qawaʿid al-Fiqh*. Karachi: Al-Sadaf Publishers, 1986.

Al-Bayhaqī, Aḥmad ibn al-Ḥusayn. *al-Sunan al-Kubrā*. Ed. Muḥammad ʿAbd al-Qādir ʿAṭā. Makkah: Maktabat Dār al-Baz, 1993.

Al-Bukhārī, ʿAlāʾ al-Dīn ʿAbd al-ʿAzīz. *Kashf al-Asrār Sharḥ Uṣūl al-Bazdāwī*. Beirut: Dār al-Kitāb al-ʿArabī, 1974.

Al-Bukhārī, Muḥammad ibn Ismāʿīl. *Ṣaḥīḥ al-Bukhārī*. Ed. Muṣṭafā al-Bughā. 3rd ed. Beirut: Dār Ibn Kathīr wa al-Yamāmah, 1986.

Al-Dihlawī, Shah Walī Allāh. *Ḥujjat Allāh al-Bālighah*. Ed. Sayyid Sābi. Beirut: Dār al-Jīl, 2005.

Al-Dāraquṭnī, ʿAlī ibn Aḥmad. *Sunan al-Dāraquṭnī*. Ed. ʿAbd Allāh Hāshim Yamānī al-Madanī. Beirut: Dār al-Maʿrifah, 1966.

Al-Dārimī, ʿAbd Allāh ibn ʿAbd al-Raḥmān. *Sunan al-Dārimī*. Ed. Fawwāz Aḥmad Zammarlī and Khālid al-Sabʿ al-ʿAlamī. Beirut: Dār al-Kitāb al-ʿArabī, 1986.

Al-Dimyāṭī, Abū Bakr ibn al-Sayyid Muḥammad Shata. *Iʿānat al-Ṭālibīn*. Beirut: Dār al-Fikr, n.d.

Al-Ghazālī, Muḥammad. *Naẓarāt fī al-Qur'ān*. 6 October City, Egypt: Nahḍat Miṣr, 2002.

Al-Ghazālī, Abū Ḥāmid Muḥammad ibn Muḥammad. *Maḥakk al-Naẓar*. Cairo: al-Matba'ah al-Adabiyyah, n.d.

Al-Ghazālī, Abū Ḥāmid Muḥammad ibn Muḥammad. *Maqāṣid al-Falāsifah*. Cairo: Dār al-Ma'rif, 1961.

Al-Ghazālī, Abū Ḥāmid Muḥammad ibn Muḥammad. *al-Mustaṣfā*. Ed. Muḥammad 'Abd al-Salām 'Abd al-Shāfī. Beirut: Dār al-Kutub al-'Ilmiyyah, 1992.

Al-Ghazālī, Abū Ḥāmid Muḥammad ibn Muḥammad. *Shifā' al-Ghalīl fī Bayān al-Shubah wa al-Makhīl wa Masālik al-Ta'alīl*. Ed. Ḥamdī al-Kubaysī. Baghdad: Maṭba'at al-Irshād, 1971.

al-Ḥākim al-Naysābūrī, Muḥammad ibn 'Abd Allāh. *al-Mustadrak 'alā al-Ṣaḥīḥayn*. Ed. Muṣṭafā 'Abd al-Qādir 'Aṭā'. Beirut: Dār al-Kutub al-'Ilmiyyah, 1990.

al-Ḥakīm al-Tirmidhī, Muḥammad ibn 'Alī. *Ithbāt al-'Ilal*. Ed. Khalid Zuhrī. Rabat: Faculty of Literature and Humanities, Muḥammad V University, 1998.

Al-Ḥanafī, Yūsuf ibn Mūsā. *Mu'tasar al-Mukhtaṣar*. Cairo: 'Ālam al-Kutub, n.d.

Ḥammād, Nāfidh Ḥusayn. *Mukhtalaf al-Ḥadīth Bayn al-Fuqahā' wa al-Muḥaddithīn*. Manṣūra, Egypt: Dār al-Wafā', 1993.

Ḥasab Allāh, 'Alī. *Uṣūl al-Tashrī' al-Islāmī*. Cairo: Dār al-Ma'ārif, 1964.

Al-Ḥāzimī, Abū Bakr. *al-I'tibār fī al-Nāsikh wa al-Mansūkh fī al-Ḥadīth*. Ed. Aḥmad Ṭantāwī and Jawharī Musaddad. Beirut: al-Maktabah al-Makkiyyah, Dār Ibn Ḥazm, 2001.

Ibn 'Abd al-Barr, Yūsuf ibn 'Abd Allāh. *al-Istidhkār*. Ed. 'Abd al-Mu'ṭī Qal'ajī. Cairo: Dār al-Wa'i; Damascus: Dār Qutaybah, n.d.

Ibn 'Abd al-Barr, Yūsuf ibn 'Abd Allāh. *al-Tamhīd*. Ed. Muḥammad ibn Aḥmad al-'Alawī and Muḥammad 'Abd al-Kabīr al-Bakrī. [Rabat]: Ministry of Public Endowments, 1967.

Ibn Abī Ḥātim, 'Abd al-Raḥmān. *al-Jarḥ wa al-Ta'dīl*. Beirut: Dār Iḥyā' al-Turāth al-'Arabī, 1952.

Ibn Amīr al-Ḥajj. *al-Taqrīr wa al-Taḥbīr*. Beirut: Dār al-Fikr, 1996.

Ibn al-'Arabī, Abū Bakr Muḥammad ibn 'Abd Allāh. *Aḥkām al-Qur'ān*. Ed. Muḥammad 'Abd al-Qādir 'Aṭā'. Beirut: Dār al-Fikr, n.d.

Ibn al-'Arabī, Abū Bakr Muḥammad ibn 'Abd Allāh. *'Aridat al-Ahwadhī*. Cairo: Dār al-Waḥy al-Muḥammadī, n.d.

Ibn 'Āshūr, Muḥammad al-Ṭāhir. *Maqāṣid al-Shari'ah al-Islāmiyyah*. Ed. Muḥammad al-Maysawī. Kuala Lumpur: Dār al-Fajr; Amman: Dār al-Nafā'is, 1999.

Ibn al-Barazī. *Nāsikh al-Qur'ān wa Mansūkhuh*. Ed. Ḥātim Ṣaliḥ al-Ḍāmin. Beirut: Mu'assasat al-Risālah, 1985.

Ibn al-Ḍaḥḥāk, Aḥmad ibn 'Amr, al-Shaybānī. *al-Āḥād wa al-Mathānī*. Ed. Bāsim al-Jawābirah. Riyadh: Dār al-Rayah, 1990.

Ibn Ḥajar al-'Asqalānī. *Fatḥ al-Bārī Sharḥ Ṣaḥīḥ al-Bukhārī*. Ed. Muḥibb al-Dīn al-Khaṭīb. Beirut: Dār al-Ma'rifah, n.d.

Ibn Ḥanbal, Aḥmad. *Musnad al-Imām Aḥmad*. Cairo: Mu'assasat Qurṭubah, n.d.

Ibn Ḥazm, 'Alī ibn Aḥmad. *al-Nāsikh wa al-Mansūkh*. Ed. 'Abd al-Ghaffār Sulaymān al-Bandārī. Beirut: Dār al-Kutub al-'Ilmiyyah, 1986.

Ibn Ḥazm, 'Alī ibn Aḥmad. *al-Iḥkām fī Uṣūl al-Aḥkām*. Cairo: Dār al-Ḥadīth, 1984.

Ibn Ḥibbān, Muḥammad, al-Tamīmī al-Bistī. *Ṣaḥīḥ Ibn Ḥibbān*. Ed. Shu'ayb al-Arna'ūṭ. 2nd ed. Beirut: Mu'assasat al-Risālah, 1993.

Ibn al-Jārūd, ʻAbd Allāh ibn ʻAlī. *al-Muntaqā min al-Sunan al-Musnadah*. Ed. ʻAbd Allāh ʻUmar al-Bārūdī. Beirut: Mu'assasat al-Kitāb al-Thaqafiyyah, 1988.

Ibn Kathīr, Ismāʻīl ibn ʻUmar. *Ikhtiṣār ʻUlūm al-Ḥadīth*. Commentary by Aḥmad Maḥmūd Shākir. Cairo: Maktabat Subayh, n.d.

Ibn Kathīr, Ismāʻīl ibn ʻUmar. *Tafsīr al-Qur'ān al-ʻAẓīm*. Beirut: Dār al-Fikr, 1981.

Ibn Kathīr, Ismāʻīl ibn ʻUmar. *Tuḥfat al-Ṭālib*. Ed. ʻAbd al-Ghanī al-Kubaysī. Makkah: Dār Hirā', 1986.

Ibn Mājah, Muḥammad ibn Yazīd. *Sunan Ibn Mājah*. Ed. Muḥammad Fu'ād ʻAbd al-Bāqī. Beirut: Dār al-Fikr, n.d.

Ibn Qayyim al-Jawziyyah, Muḥammad ibn Abī Bakr. *Iʻlām al-Muwaqqiʻīn ʻan Rabb al-ʻĀlamīn*. Ed. Ṭāhā ʻAbd al-Ra'ūf Saʻd. Beirut: Dār al-Jīl, 1973.

Ibn Qayyim al-Jawziyyah, Muḥammad ibn Abī Bakr. *Zād al-Maʻād fī Hady Khayr al-ʻIbād*. Ed. Shuʻayb al-Arna'ūṭ and ʻAbd al-Qādir al-Arna'ūṭ. 8th ed. Beirut: Mu'assasat al-Risālah, n.d.

Ibn Qudāmah, ʻAbd Allāh ibn Aḥmad, al-Maqdisī. *al-Mughnī*. Beirut: Dār al-Fikr, 1985.

Ibn Qudāmah, ʻAbd Allāh ibn Aḥmad, al-Maqdisī. *Rawḍat al-Nāẓir*. Ed. ʻAbd al-ʻAzīz ʻAbd al-Raḥmān al-Saʻīd. 2nd ed. Riyadh: Jāmiʻat Imam Muḥammad ibn Saʻūd, 1979.

Ibn Qutaybah, ʻAbd Allāh ibn Muslim. *Ta'wīl Mukhtalaf al-Ḥadīth*. Ed. Muḥammad Zuhrī al-Najjār. Beirut: Dār al-Jīl, 1973.

Ibn Rushd, Muḥammad ibn Aḥmad. *Bidāyat al-Mujtahid wa Nihāyat al-Muqtaṣid*. Beirut: Dār al-Fikr, n.d.

Ibn Taymiyyah, Aḥmad ʻAbd al-Ḥalīm. *Dar' Taʻāruḍ al-ʻAql wa al-Naql*. Beirut: Dār al-Kutub al-ʻIlmiyyah, 1997.

Ibn Taymiyyah, Aḥmad ʻAbd al-Ḥalīm. *Kutub wa Rasā'il wa Fatāwā Ibn Taymiyyah fī al-Fiqh*. Ed. ʻAbd al-Raḥmān ibn

Muḥammad al-'Āṣimī al-Najdī. 2nd ed. N.p.: Maktabat Ibn Taymiyyah, n.d.

Ibn Taymiyyah, Aḥmad 'Abd al-Ḥalīm. *al-Muswaddah fī Uṣūl al-Fiqh*. Ed. Muḥammad Muḥyī al-Dīn 'Abd al-Ḥamīd. Cairo: Dār al-Madanī, n.d.

'Īsā, 'Abd al-Jalīl. *Ijtihād al-Rasūl*. Kuwait: Dār al-Bayān, 1984.

Jābir, Ḥasan. *al-Maqāṣid al-Kulliyyah lil-Shar' wa al-Ijtihād al-Mu'āṣir*. Beirut: Dār al-Ḥiwār, 2001.

Al-Jassās, Aḥmad ibn 'Alī. *Ahkam al-Qur'ān*. Ed. Muḥammad al-Ṣādiq Qamhāwī. Beirut: Dār Iḥyā' al-Turāth al-'Arabī, 1985.

Al-Jassās, Aḥmad ibn 'Alī. *al-Fuṣūl fī al-Uṣūl*. Ed. Ujayl al-Nashmi. Kuwait: Ministry of Endowments, 1985.

Jughaym, Nu'mān. *Ṭuruq al-Kashf 'an Maqāṣid al-Shari'*. Amman: Dār al-Nafā'is, 2002.

Al-Juwaynī, Abū al-Ma'ālī 'Abd al-Malik ibn 'Abd Allāh. *al-Burhan fī Uṣūl al-Fiqh*. Ed. 'Abd al-'Aẓīm al-Dīb. 4th ed. Manṣūra, Egypt: Dār al-Wafā', 1997.

Al-Juwaynī, Abū al-Ma'ālī 'Abd al-Malik ibn 'Abd Allāh. *Ghiyāth al-Umam fī Iltiyāth al-Ẓulam*. Ed. 'Abd al-'Aẓīm al-Dīb. Doha: Ministry of Religious Affairs, 1980.

Al-Karmī, Mir'ī. *Qalā'id al-Marjān fī Bayān al-Nāsikh wa al-Mansūkh fī al-Qur'ān*. Ed. Sāmī 'Aṭā Ḥasan. Kuwait: Dār al-Qur'ān al-Karīm, n.d.

Ibn Khayyāṭ, Usāmah. *Mukhtalaf al-Ḥadīth Bayn al-Muḥaddithūn wa al-Uṣūliyyīn al-Fuqahā'*. N.p.: Dār al-Faḍīlah, 2001.

Al-Khuḍarī Bik, Muḥammad. *Uṣūl al-Fiqh*. N.p.: al-Maktabah al-Tijāriyyah al-Kubrā, 1389/1969.

Al-Maghribī, Muḥammad ibn Muḥammad ibn 'Abd al-Raḥmān. *Mawāhib al-Jalīl li-Sharḥ Mukhtaṣar Khalīl*. 2nd ed. Beirut: Dār al-Fikr, 1978.

Malik ibn Anas al-Aṣbaḥī. *al-Muwaṭṭa'*. Ed. Muḥammad Fu'ād 'Abd al-Bāqī. Cairo: Dār Iḥyā' al-Turāth al-'Arabī, n.d.

Al-Maqdisī, Muḥammad ibn Ṭāhir. *Dhakhīrat al-Ḥuffāẓ*. Ed. 'Abd al-Raḥmān al-Firyuwai. Riyadh: Dār al-Salaf, 1996.

Al-Mubārakfūrī, Muḥammad 'Abd al-Raḥmān. *Tuḥfat al-Aḥwadhī*. Beirut: Dār al-Kutub al-'Ilmiyyah, n.d.

Muslim ibn al-Ḥajjāj. *Ṣaḥīḥ Muslim*. Ed. Muḥammad Fu'ād 'Abd al-Bāqī. Beirut: Dār Iḥyā' al-Turāth al-'Arabī, n.d.

Nadā, Muḥammad Maḥmūd. *al-Naskh fī al-Qur'ān Bayn al-Mu'ayyidīn wa al-Mu'āriḍīn*. Cairo: al-Dār al-'Arabīyyah lil-Kitāb, 1996.

Al-Naḥḥās, Aḥmad ibn Muḥammad. *al-Nāsikh wa al-Mansūkh*. Ed. Muḥammad 'Abd al-Salām Muḥammad. Kuwait: Maktabat al-Falāḥ, 1408/1988.

Al-Nasā'ī, Aḥmad ibn Shu'ayb. *al-Sunan al-Kubrā*. Ed. 'Abd al-Ghaffar al-Bandarī and Sayyid Ḥasan. Beirut: Dār al-Kutub al-'Ilmiyyah, 1990.

Al-Nawawī, Yaḥyā ibn Sharaf. *al-Majmū'*. Beirut: Dār al-Fikr, 1997.

Al-Nawawī, Yaḥyā ibn Sharaf. *Sharḥ al-Nawawī 'alā Ṣaḥīḥ Muslim*. 2nd ed. Beirut: Dār Iḥyā' al-Turāth al-'Arabī, 1972.

Al-Qaradāwī, Yūsuf. *Fiqh al-Zakāt*. 15th ed. Cairo, Mu'assasat al-Risālah, 1985.

Al-Qaradāwī, Yūsuf. *Madkhal li-Dirāsat al-Sharī'ah al-Islāmiyyah*. 3rd ed. Cairo: Maktabat Wahbah, 1997.

Al-Qarafī, Aḥmad ibn Idrīs. *al-Dhakhīrah*. Ed. Muḥammad Ḥājjī. Beirut: Dār al-Gharb, 1994.

Al-Qurṭubī, Muḥammad ibn Aḥmad. *Tafsīr al-Qurṭubī*. Cairo: Dār al-Sha'b, n.d.

Al-Rāzī, Fakhr al-Dīn Muḥammad ibn 'Umar. *al-Maḥṣūl*. Ed. Ṭāhā Jābir al-Alwānī. Riyadh: Imam Muḥammad ibn Sa'ūd University, 1980.

Al-Rāzī, Fakhr al-Dīn Muḥammad ibn 'Umar. *al-Tafsīr al-Kabīr aw Mafātīḥ al-Ghayb*. Beirut: Dār al-Kutub al-'Ilmiyyah, 2000.

Al-Rāzī, Muḥammad ibn Abī Bakr. *Mukhtār al-Ṣiḥāḥ*. Ed. Maḥmūd Khaṭīr. Beirut: Maktabat Lubnān, 1994.

Al-Sa'dī, 'Abd al-Ḥakīm. *Mabāḥith al-'Illah fī al-Qiyās 'Ind al-Uṣūliyyīn*. Beirut: Dār al-Basha'ir al-Islāmiyyah, 1986.

Al-Sadūsī, Qatādah ibn Di'āmah. *al-Nāsikh wa al-Mansūkh*. Ed. Ḥātim Ṣaliḥ al-Ḍāmin, Mu'assasat al-Risālah, 1998.

Al-Sadūsī, Qatadah et al. *Silsilat Kutub al-Nāsikh wa al-Mansūkh*. Ed. Ḥātim Salih al-Ḍāmin. Beirut: Mu'assasat al-Risālah, 2000.

Al-Sam'ānī, Manṣūr ibn Muḥammad. *Qawāṭi' al-Adillah fī al-Uṣūl*. Ed. Muḥammad Ḥasan al-Shafie. Beirut: Dār al-Kutub al-'Ilmiyyah, 1997.

Al-Ṣan'ānī, Muḥammad ibn Ismā'īl al-Amīr. *Subul al-Salām*. Ed. Muḥammad 'Abd al-Azīz al-Khūlī. 4th ed. Beirut: Dār Iḥyā' al-Turāth al-'Arabī, 1959.

Al-Sarakhsī, Muḥammad ibn Aḥmad. *Uṣūl al-Sarakhsī*. Beirut: Dār al-Ma'rifah, n.d.

Al-Sawsawah, 'Abd al-Majīd. *Minhāj al-Tawfīq wa al-Tarjīḥ Bayn Mukhtalaf al-Ḥadīth*. Amman: Dār al-Nafā'is, 1997.

Al-Shāfi'ī, Muḥammad ibn Idrīs. *Ikhtilāf al-Ḥadīth*. Ed. Amīr Aḥmad Ḥaydar. Beirut: Mu'assasat al-Kutub, 1985.

Al-Shāfi'ī, Muḥammad ibn Idrīs. *Musnad al-Shāfi'ī*. Beirut: Dār al-Kutub al-'Ilmiyyah, n.d.

Al-Shāfi'ī, Muḥammad ibn Idrīs. *al-Risālah*. Ed. Aḥmad Shakir. Cairo: Dār al-Fikr and al-Madanī, 1939.

Al-Shāfi'ī, Muḥammad ibn Idrīs. *al-Umm*. 2nd ed. Beirut: Dār al-Ma'rifah, 1973.

Al-Shāṭibī, Ibrāhīm ibn Mūsā. *al-Muwāfaqāt*. Ed. 'Abd Allāh Drāz. Beirut: Dār al-Ma'rifah, n.d.

Al-Shawkānī, Muḥammad ibn 'Alī. *Fatḥ al-Qadīr*. Beirut: Dār al-Fikr, n.d.

Al-Shawkānī, Muḥammad ibn 'Alī. *Irshād al-Fuḥūl ilā Taḥqīq al-Ḥaqq min 'Ilm al-Uṣūl*. Ed. Muḥammad Sa'īd al-Badrī. Beirut: Dār al-Fikr, 1991.

Al-Shawkānī, Muḥammad ibn 'Alī. *Nayl al-Awṭār*. Beirut: Dār al-Jīl, 1973.

Al-Shīrāzī, Ibrāhīm ibn 'Alī. *al-Luma' fī Uṣūl al-Fiqh*. Beirut: Dār al-Kutub al-'Ilmiyyah, 1985.

Al-Subkī, 'Abd al-Wahhāb ibn 'Alī. *al-Ashbah wa al-Naẓā'ir*. Ed. 'Alī Mu'awwad and 'Ādil 'Abd al-Mawjūd. Beirut: Dār al-Kutub al-'Ilmiyyah, 1991.

Al-Subkī, 'Alī ibn 'Abd al-Kāfī and Tāj al-Dīn. *al-Ibhāj Sharḥ al-Minhāj*. Beirut: Dār al-Kutub al-'Ilmiyyah, 1984.

Sulṭān, Ṣalāḥ al-Dīn 'Abd al-Ḥalīm. *Ḥujjiyyāt al-Adillah al-Ijtihādiyyah al-Mukhtalaf 'alayhā fī al-Sharī'at al-Islāmīyyah*. Ph.D. thesis. Cairo: University of Cairo, Department of Islamic Law, 1992.

Al-Suyūṭī, 'Abd al-Raḥmān ibn Abī Bakr. *'Ayn al-Iṣābah fī Istidrāk 'Ā'ishah 'alā al-Ṣaḥābah*. Cairo: Maktabat al-'Ilm, 1988.

Al-Suyūṭī, 'Abd al-Raḥmān ibn Abī Bakr. *al-Itqān fī 'Ulūm al-Qur'ān*. Cairo: al-Maṭba'ah al-Azhariyyah al-Miṣriyyah, 1900.

Al-Suyūṭī, 'Abd al-Raḥmān ibn Abī Bakr. *Tadrīb al-Rāwī*. Ed. 'Abd al-Wahhāb 'Abd al-Laṭīf. Madīnah: al-Maktabah al-'Ilmiyyah, 1972.

Al-Ṭabarānī, Sulaymān ibn Aḥmad. *al-Mu'jam al-Awsaṭ*. Ed. Ṭāriq ibn 'Awaḍ Allāh Muḥammad and 'Abd al-Muḥsin al-Ḥusaynī. Cairo: Dār al-Ḥaramayn, 1994.

Al-Ṭabarānī, Sulaymān ibn Aḥmad. *al-Mu'jam al-Kabīr*. Ed. Ḥamdī ibn 'Abd al-Majīd al-Salafī. 2nd ed. Mosul: Maktabat al-'Ulūm wa al-Ḥikam, 1984.

Al-Ṭabarānī, Sulaymān ibn Aḥmad. *Musnad al-Shāmiyyīn*. Ed. Ḥamdī ibn 'Abd al-Majīd al-Salafī. Beirut: Mu'assasat al-Risālah, 1985.

Al-Ṭabarī, Muḥammad ibn Jarīr. *Jāmi' al-Bayān 'an Ta'wīl Āy al-Qur'ān*. Beirut: Dār al-Fikr, 1985.

Al-Ṭaḥāwī, Aḥmad ibn Muḥammad. *Sharḥ Ma'ānī al-Āthār*. Ed. Muḥammad Zuhrī al-Najjār. Beirut: Dār al-Kutub al-'Ilmiyyah, 1979.

Al-Tamīmī, Abū Ya'lā Aḥmad ibn 'Alī. *Musnad Abī Ya'lā*. Ed. Ḥusayn Salīm Asad. Damascus: Dār al-Ma'mūn lil-Turāth, 1984.

Al-Tirmidhī, Muḥammad ibn 'Īsā. *Sunan al-Tirmidhī*. Ed. Aḥmad Muḥammad Shākir et al. Beirut: Dār Iḥyā' al-Turāth al-'Arabī, n.d.

Al-Ṭūfī, Sulaymān ibn 'Abd al-Qawī. *al-Ta'yīn fī Sharḥ al-Arba'īn*. Beirut: Mu'assasat al-Rayyān, 1998.

Al-Turābī, Ḥasan. *Qaḍāyā al-Tajdīd: Naḥw Minhāj Uṣūlī*. Beirut: Dār al-Hādī, 2000.

Zayd, Muṣṭafā. *al-Naskh fī al-Qur'ān al-Karīm*. Cairo: Dār al-Fikr al-'Arabī, 1963.

Al-Zurqānī, 'Abd al-'Aẓīm. *Manāhil al-'Irfān*. Cairo: 'Īsā al-Bābī al-Ḥalabī, n.d.

Al-Zurqānī, Muḥammad ibn 'Abd al-Bāqī ibn Yūsuf. *Sharḥ al-Zurqānī 'alā al-Muwaṭṭa'*. Beirut: Dār al-Kutub al-'Ilmiyyah, 1990.

Index